KNIGHT ERRANT

A MEMOIR OF WORLD WAR II

⚜

Knight Errant
A Bank Clerk Goes to War

A MEMOIR OF WORLD WAR II

⚜

by
ROBERT IRWIN KNIGHT

Edited and with an Introduction by DERMOT SCOTT

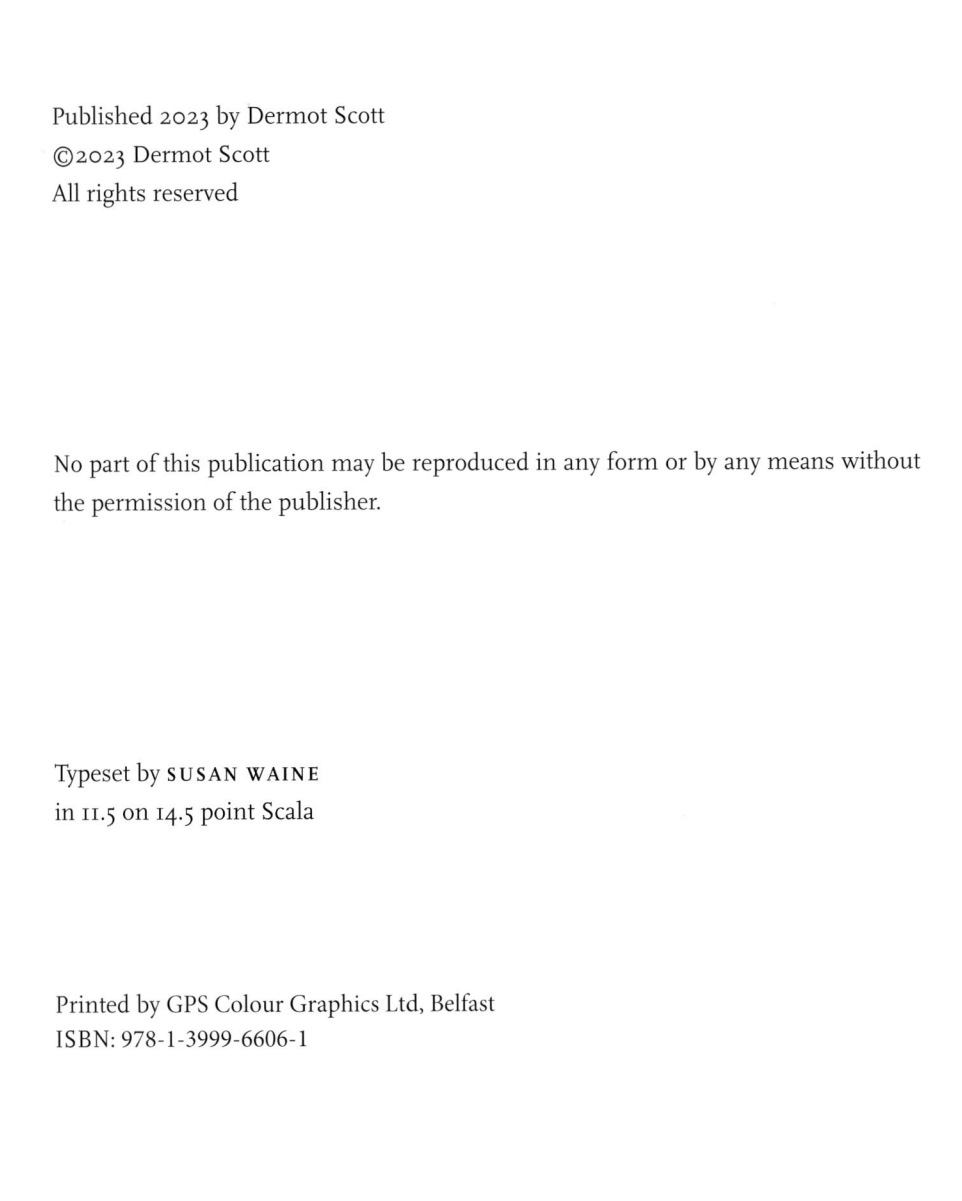

Published 2023 by Dermot Scott
©2023 Dermot Scott
All rights reserved

No part of this publication may be reproduced in any form or by any means without the permission of the publisher.

Typeset by SUSAN WAINE
in 11.5 on 14.5 point Scala

Printed by GPS Colour Graphics Ltd, Belfast
ISBN: 978-1-3999-6606-1

CONTENTS

Glossary		6
Introduction		7
1	**JOINING UP**	17
	3 May 1939	18
	3 September 1939	26
	France 21 December 1939	35
2	**THE RETREAT**	43
	10 May 1940	43
	28 May 1940: HMS Montrose	50
3	**FROM DUNKIRK TO THE INVASION 1940-1944**	58
	Autumn-Winter 1940-41: Coventry, London Blitz, Stockton	58
	Spring 1941; Commissioned Officer: Wales, Gourock	63
	Colleagues	68
	1942-44: Training for the invasion	74
	London society	76
4	**THE RETURN 1944-1945**	78
	22 June 1944 (D Day +16); landing in Normandy	80
	July-August 1944: Break-Out. Rouen. The French	83
	Towards the Low Countries	88
	September 1944: Belgium, Ghent, Brussels, Antwerp	90
	Late September 1944: Operation Market Garden, the Netherlands. Nijmegen	92
	Winter 1944-45; the Rhine	95
	March 1945: Germany. Army of Occupation	103
	1945: Aftermath. New challenges	109
	Postscript	115
	Acknowledgements	116

GLOSSARY

AA	Anti-Aircraft ("Ack-Ack")	OTC	Officer Training Corps
AckIG	(=Ast IG?) Assistant Instructor in Gunnery	Pioneer	soldiers undertaking construction
ATS	Auxiliary Territorial Service	PSI	Permanent Staff Instructor
BEF	British Expeditionary Force	PT	Physical Training
BRA	Belfast Royal Academy	RA	Royal Artillery
CO	Commanding Officer	RA structure	HQ Battery; 2 Batteries: 2 Troops 4 guns each
HAA	Heavy Anti-Aircraft		
HAC	Honorable Artillery Company	RE	Royal Engineers
HMS	His Majesty's Ship	RHQ	Regimental Headquarters
I/C	In command	RTO	Railway Traffic Officer
IG	Instructor in Gunnery	Shankill	Protestant working class area of Belfast
IRA	Irish Republican Army		
KC	King's Counsel	SR	Supplementary Reserve
L/Bdr	Lance Bombardier	TCD	Trinity College Dublin
MC	Military Cross	The Monk	Irwin's nickname (from Monk's Ale)
MO	Medical Officer		
NAAFI	Navy, Army and Air Force Institutes (catering)	Tir-na-nÒg	Land of the Ever-Young (Irish mythology; house name)
NCO	Non-Commissioned Officer	YMCA	Young Men's Christian Organisation
OCTU	Officer Cadets Training Unit		
OP or O/P	Observation Post		

INTRODUCTION

ROBERT IRWIN KNIGHT, 22 NOVEMBER 1914 – 9 DECEMBER 2004

Irwin Knight was a teacher and raconteur, steeped in English literature, who spent the best part of his life inspiring his pupils at Banbridge Academy with a feeling for drama, poetry and prose. Equally at home with Chaucer and Beckett, Shakespeare and Austen, he found in them a constant source of reference and of pleasure.

His career as a teacher was his third; his previous lives had been as a bank clerk and a soldier. Employment in the bank he regarded as a penance that he was delighted to shrug off, the army as a duty. His military service was a source of bafflement, exhilaration, discomfort, anxiety, shame and eventual satisfaction, not least in that it gave him the confidence to change direction, undertake a degree course and enter the teaching profession.

This civilised, witty and charming man could write well, and we are fortunate to have his memoir of service in world war two. In retirement, some forty years after the events, he recounted vivid details of his experiences and associated them with episodes in literature that he had absorbed in the intervening years. Written originally for his nephews and nieces, the memoir now seems to them, twenty years after his death, to be worth wider circulation. The following biographical note aims to set the memoir in context.

Robert Irwin Knight, known always as Irwin, was born in Glenburn Park, Belfast in November 1914, the eldest son and second child of John Radcliffe Knight and Mary Lindsay Knight (née Armstrong). His elder sister Florence ("Bee") was born in

ABOVE:
Irwin aged 15

RIGHT:
Cycling, aged 18

1910 and his younger twin brothers Jack and Lindsay in 1918. In 1926 the family moved to *Tir-na-nÒg*, 5 Castle Park, at the top of Cavehill Road. Here they had immediate access to the slopes of the Cave Hill and the grounds of Belfast Castle, and there Irwin developed his love of the natural world. Irwin, like his siblings, attended Belfast Royal Academy, the oldest school in the city of Belfast, a co-educational, non-denominational voluntary grammar school with, then and still, a notably liberal ethos. Irwin was Head Boy, and played on the first XV.

His father, John Radcliffe Knight, who sprang from a large, artisan, Banbridge family, left school at fourteen years and entered Gallahers, then a small tobacco enterprise and, later, a

INTRODUCTION

very large one. He remained with the firm throughout his working life, ending his career as chief cashier and head office manager. He was clearly much appreciated by the owner and chairman Thomas Gallaher who, when the firm went public in the 1920s, gave him a substantial sum with which to pay off the debt on his new house.

Irwin's mother, Mary Armstrong (known as May), whom Irwin describes as coming from a "better social background" and as "a most able person", encouraged her husband to rise in the firm. This he did. "By his innocence", Irwin writes, "lack of guile, absolute integrity and friendliness he won the warmest affection and respect of all those who had the intelligence to appreciate him." Besides his career in Gallahers, his main interests were Fortwilliam Presbyterian Church, of which he was an elder, and the Masonic Order, where he rose to the rank of Prince Mason.

In the early 1930s Irwin obtained a post in the Northern Bank, a secure and pensionable job prized especially in this period of widespread poverty and precarious employment. He worked first in a rural branch of the bank in Fivemileown, with colleagues he later described as likeable drunks and gamblers. The *Impartial Reporter* records that, on 11 June 1936, he was runner-up in the Fivemiletown President's Cup for golf, awarded by Sir Basil Brooke, the local landlord and MP. Irwin was later transferred to Downpatrick which he thoroughly disliked, in particular for its snobbish bank manager.

THE MEMOIR

The memoir begins in early 1939 when Irwin volunteered for the Territorial Army. On 1 April he joined the Royal Artillery, 8th (Belfast) Heavy Anti Aircraft Regiment, and was mobilised on 25 August. Jack joined at the same time, enlisting in the same regiment but, on Irwin's advice, in a different Battery; Lindsay had already been active in the Queen's University Officers' Training Corps (OTC). After some months of training, Irwin's unit landed at Le Havre just before Christmas 1939 to join the

British Expeditionary Force. By 1 April 1940, the anniversary of the regiment's establishment, they were dug in about 5km southeast of Arras.

On 10 May 1940 the phoney war ended and a period of confusion began that lasted until he arrived back in England via the beaches of Dunkirk. This chaotic period is fully and vividly described in his memoir.

All three brothers having been evacuated from different points on the coast of France, they met in London later in 1940 for the first and only time during the war. Jack was to spend several years fighting the Japanese in India and Burma, while Lindsay's war, in the North Irish Horse, took him with the 8th Army to North Africa and Italy, where he was wounded and where he was decorated for gallantry. Irwin spent the next four years in England despite volunteering for service overseas. During this much less dramatic period in his wartime experience, the memoir hints at a high-society romance in London, and two important events took place: he became a Commissioned officer; and he came to the decision that he would prefer, on eventually returning to civil life, to resign his job in the Northern Bank and take a university degree. As he wrestled with this decision, he wrote for advice to his sister Bee, married to Eric Scott, a Presbyterian Minister in Ramelton.

In the final chapter he recounts his part in the Normandy campaign, and in Belgium, Netherlands and Germany. This too is told with remarkable insight and sympathy for the liberated population. The end of war brought worry and apprehension, problems which he eventually resolved.

Throughout the text are numerous pen-pictures, sympathetic, ribald or caustic, of private soldiers, officers, the civilians he liberates, rich and poor, and the defeated. His sympathies are consistently with the less fortunate, reflecting perhaps his own feelings of inadequacy and social inferiority. These feelings, whether deserved or not, are emphasised at frequent intervals in the text, and contrast with his actual achievements both during the war and later.

INTRODUCTION

POST-WAR

All three brothers survived the war and returned to Belfast. Their parents were of course overjoyed at their safe return, although their mother found her good fortune sometimes embarrassing when encountering those of her friends who had lost a son. Jack soon took a post in local government. Lindsay found employment, like his father, in Gallahers, and was posted to Rhodesia; however he soon married and with the encouragement of his in-laws took a position with the new Courtaulds business in Carrickfergus outside Belfast. Irwin on the other hand, encouraged by his sister Bee and by Professor R L Marshall, Bee's brother-in-law, did in fact quit his secure post in the Northern Bank and begin a degree course, funded – sparsely – by his savings and military gratuity. Professor Marshall not only encouraged him to do so, but offered him board and lodging at his college, Magee College in Londonderry, where it was possible to take the first two years of the four-year honours degree course at Trinity College Dublin. Professor Marshall and his wife provided accommodation on-campus and the professor provided intensive tutoring in English, an invaluable perk for a man returning to study at the age of 32 after the stress and distractions of war, and something that Irwin valued immensely.

The final two years of the course were spent at Trinity, with long vacations at his parents' home in Belfast. He appears to have kept much to himself in Dublin, perhaps from shortage of funds and perhaps from lack of empathy with the generally young and frivolous student population that lacked his experience of the war. The neutral status of the Republic during the war left him out of sympathy with the local ethos.

He enjoyed the academic course, worked intensively at his books and graduated with a First-Class Honours degree in Modern Languages, in his case English and French. Thereafter, in preparation to apply for a teaching post in Northern Ireland, he took a position of *assistant* at a secondary school in France and spent an uncomfortable nine months at an *Ecole Normale* in Brittany.

TEACHER

On return to Ireland he applied for and gained a teaching post at Banbridge Academy, a school that had several attractions. The headmaster was Dr William Haughton Crowe, a family friend whose son Michael had been Irwin's contemporary at Trinity; and for some years he lived with the Crowes at Ballievey House, a former "Bleacher's house". Another attraction was the return to family roots: his grandfather Knight, originally employed in the linen industry, had moved from Banbridge to Belfast in the mid-nineteenth century.

When Irwin's father died in 1951 his mother lived on in Castle Park with her son Jack. For some time Irwin commuted by bus daily to Banbridge, having set the fire and made the breakfast, returning in the evening by the same route. Jack married Jane Morrison in 1955 and they lived with his mother until her death in early 1959; Irwin paid sincere tribute to their care for her in her declining years. Meanwhile, Irwin fell in love with Helen Shilliday, a medical doctor, and married her in June 1959, having delayed this event to offer continued support to his mother.

Irwin was immensely satisfied with his life as a teacher, and this satisfaction was reciprocated by his pupils among whom most, if not all, seem to have held him in esteem and affection. James Simpson, the writer, who was a pupil at the Academy from 1964-1971, recalled "the late Irwin Knight, then the highly-respected head of English... a wonderful teacher, with a lovely sense of humour... He had star quality as a professional and a human being... He made me believe that I could write. He gave me the English prize and boosted my self-esteem. I owe him and the Academy a great deal."

Alva Brangam writes: "Irwin was, quite simply, a model of the perfect teacher, and I know many former pupils from a number of different school generations would agree. He managed to inspire interest in his subject, preserve discipline, hold attention, encourage private study and achieve exceptional examination results whilst working towards the educational and social development of his pupils. He was an all rounder in class, on the dramatic society stage or the touch-line.

With Irwin learning seemed to be fun. He conditioned my choice of career and University. Whilst I was an undergraduate we corresponded and beyond school we became firm friends."

Irwin once remarked that probably the most brilliant pupil he taught was Harden Rodgers, daughter of the poet WR Rodgers, and later Scholar of Trinity and lecturer in English; but he also observed that his greatest satisfaction as a teacher was to see awakening a glimmer of literary appreciation in the eyes of an unpromising pupil.

He retired in 1979 and survived, in excellent mental health, to celebrate his ninetieth birthday in 2004. During his retirement his three great loves were his wife Helen, their garden, and the stream of former pupils who came to visit him, from near and far.

A NOTE ON THE TEXT

The memoir was originally typed by Irwin between October 1981 and January 1982, some forty years after the events it describes. A clean copy was retyped in November 2020 at the instigation of Mary Howie, his niece. The text as published is largely unchanged: some repetition between chapters has been corrected and the punctuation has been revised; the footnotes are mine. Otherwise the only changes have been to anonymise some of the less flattering pen-pictures of his colleagues, to shorten an egregiously flattering homage to one of his heroes, and to curtail the repeated assertion of his own inadequacy. The sympathy, humanity and humour of the text, which I hope remains unspoilt, is a true reflection of the man.

DERMOT SCOTT

MEMOIR

⚜

Northern Bank,
Fivemiletown

JOINING UP I

It was probably during the Munich crisis, in September 1938, that the notion of joining some branch of the Armed Services first entered my head.

At that time I was a bank official of some four years' standing and, on a salary of £120 per annum, occupying the position of junior accountant in the Downpatrick Branch of the Northern Bank Ltd. This post penned me all day in a little cubicle, posting cheques to the A to L accounts in two massive lodgers and, by way of variety, checking the postings of the senior accountant in the even more massive ledgers of the M to Z accounts. A more monotonous occupation would be hard to find; further, it was one entirely unsuited to me for it necessitated absolute accuracy in figures, a talent which was not mine. I hated that job; I did not greatly care for some of my colleagues – they lacked the colour of the drunkards and gamblers who were my brethren in Fivemiletown, and whom I shall always remember with great affection. And I heartily detested the town of Downpatrick. Yet, had war not come, I never would have had the courage to shake off the bondage of such service and to seek a better way of life.

However, to return to the Munich crisis, Chamberlain the Prime Minister was in that German city seeking Hitler's assurance that with the annexation of the Sudetenland of Czechoslovakia, Germany's territorial ambitions were fulfilled. Everyone in the British Isles realised that Britain was faced with the choice of betraying the Czech people by acquiescing in this annexation or of declaring war on Hitler's Reich. The fateful decision was made on Friday 30 September. It is a day that lives in my memory. A day of unceasing rain, when the lights were lit early in the office, when few customers bothered us with business and we waited in the gathering darkness for the news, which could only be bad.

At last it came. War had been averted. Chamberlain declared that he had obtained from the negotiations "Peace with Honour" adding, "I believe that it is peace for our time." But it was anything but that, and even I, an insignificant bank clerk, experienced a feeling of shame that my country had been forced to act so dishonourably. The gloom of the day seemed appropriate to the darkness of the deed. Yet, to be truthful, it must be added that I felt vastly relieved that we were not to be hurled into the horrors of war. Shame and relief were the prevailing sensations in my breast, but also, there was the underlying idea that we would not so easily escape our responsibilities. I think I could best sum up my feelings that evening by echoing the words of Hamlet, "And I am sick at heart." Mind you, I did not then know these words.

While writing this first page I paused to read chapters 16-27 of volume 1 of Churchill's *Second World War*. There he gives an account of his actions and thoughts at this time. His cares were considerably more formidable than mine, and it thrilled me to read of the vastness of this man's vision; he played with millions of lives, I, unenthusiastically, with one.

In the months that followed I wondered what I should do. I knew that if war came I would join up; but I would do so not for any noble or heroic motive, but because I would be ashamed not to enlist. I knew all too well that I lacked the courage, dash and stamina of a soldier; indeed I think I thought that it would be best to get killed "for the look of the thing."

3 MAY 1939

Then in the early months of 1939, it was announced that a Brigade of Royal Artillery (Heavy and Light) Anti-Aircraft units was to be established in Northern Ireland as part of the Supplementary Reserve (subtly distinguished, in some way, from the Territorial Army). Whether or not it was hoped that the

JOINING UP

sudden expansion on the armed forces would deter Herr Hitler from any further adventures, I don't know; he certainly cannot have learned that he was soon to be faced with such a redoubtable opponent as me – otherwise... Be that as it may, on 1 April 1939 (ever remembered as All Fool's Day by the Shankill Road boys who joined), recruitment opened for the new force. Now, as enlisting seemed to me a matter of personal decision, I told no-one of my plans and so it was that, on my own, I found myself signed on at the recruiting centre in the YMCA on 3 May 1939, Army No 1463058. I cannot remember much of that occasion except that we were medically examined, signed a few documents and were told to report on a given date to the 8th HAA Regt RA (SR) (8th Heavy Anti Aircraft Regiment, Royal Artillery (Supplementary Reserve)) at Dunmore Park (the greyhound track) Antrim Road, Belfast.

So, I had joined the Supplementary Reserve and by so doing had pledged myself to appear on a certain number of parades per year, to attend an annual fortnight's camp and, in the event of an emergency, to serve as a full-time soldier. In grateful acknowledgement of my services, the War Office promised to pay me a bounty of £12 per annum and to cover my travelling expenses for attendance at parades. I should add that the Northern Bank Ltd undertook to pay me while at camp; they further agreed later to augment my service pay until such times as I was earning more as a soldier than as a bank clerk. This was a decent enough gesture; and anyway, I soon was on a higher rate of pay than while in the service of the bank.

Enlisting was a lonely experience; but to my great joy, I found that similar steps had been taken by many of my Antrim Road friends, and that close on my heels, and on their own volition, came my brother Jack and my best loved friend William John Jefferson.[1] Jack wished to join the 21st Battery, but I persuaded him that he should go into 23rd Battery; my idea being that, in

---

1 AKA Jeff, Willie, Willie John

a tight corner, one of us might be fortunate to be elsewhere. He agreed. I must here record that my brother Lindsay had, a year earlier, been admitted to the Queen's University Officers' Training Corps (OTC) and so was already training as an infantry officer. That Willie Jefferson accompanied me during my army days until, through ill-health (a detached retina) he had to resign, I count one of the greatest blessings of my life. I owe to him more that I can ever express and place him in the select company of my father and Doc Marshall. Friends who joined at that time included Charlie Jefferson, Frank Dalzell, Jack Baillie, Lynn Clements, Harry Porter and Harry McKibben (an officer).

The drills at Dunmore were held on Tuesdays and Thursdays. I eagerly welcomed them as an opportunity to escape for the evening from hated Downpatrick and to travel, free of expenses, home to Belfast. The training given us was minimal. In those first weeks most of the time was occupied in taking names and arranging for the issue of denim overalls, boots and caps, usually one item per session. We also engaged in some remarkable exercises which we later came to know as Dismounted Foot Drill. The secret underlying this performance was that the Artillery, having previously been a mounted formation, was unable to execute, because of the horses, the simple right-about turn of the infantry man. The result was that in order to complete a turn of 180 degrees it was necessary for men to fall-in in two long parallel lines and to complete a wheeling movement pivoting either on the centre or the ends of each line. As nothing of this tradition was revealed to us, confusion, chaos and frustration reigned in our ranks and our regular instructors appeared to consider us the greatest collection of morons it had been their misfortune to encounter. Happily for all, when hostilities broke out, the Royal Regiment adopted, perhaps reluctantly, the normal foot-drill of the infantry. We no longer needed to pretend that we were on horseback.

Once each month a pay parade was held to reimburse travelling expenses. Most of the lads came from Belfast and so their money was composed of shillings and pence but I came from Downpatrick so my money was much greater. The pay-sergeant gave Gunner Smith 1/10d, Gunner Brown 2/4d, Gunner Knight £6-15-6. The lads thought I came from outer space.

Sometime in July there arrived at Dunmore one 3-inch gun and a strange assortment of instruments, predictors, height finders and spotters. We did not know their names nor were we allowed to lay a hand on them. Their intricacies had first to be explained to our officers.

I should mention here that our regiment, being an entirely new formation, had no NCOs, except for the cadre of permanent staff instructors (PSIs), and so promotions came thick and fast. I became Gun Sergeant in the space of about three months; this was a scandal. I knew nothing of the job and a regular soldier usually had to serve for ten years before reaching such heights. Jeff, who had enlisted a couple of weeks later than I did, became a lance-sergeant in the same time. We came to the conclusion that if a man was able to read, write, add and subtract, he gained a stripe for each accomplishment. Still, that's hardly fair to the army selection methods; in the 8th Regt, those chosen in the early days to be NCOs, by and large, did a good job (modest fellow!) and the majority went on to obtain commissions.

During those first weeks of summer, the seriousness of the world situation hardly struck home and most of us thought, rather light-heartedly, that we had committed ourselves for four years to what would be a jolly and amusing experience. This outlook was maybe coloured by stories of the riotous goings-on at the annual Queen's OTC camps in Blackpool or Douglas. This state of euphoria however came to an abrupt end. On 25 August 1939 the order was issued for the general mobilisation of the Territorial Army. That day my world (and my tummy) turned over.

I remember that at about 9.30 in the morning I was called to the Branch telephone to hear my mother say that the regimental office had phoned to order Jack and me to report immediately to Dunmore Park. My mother had replied that I was stationed in Downpatrick and that my brother and I would present ourselves as soon as I reached Belfast. I then let my manager, Mr William Wright, know that I had been called up for army service. His reaction to my news was to tell me that I had no need to worry and that I would be back again, at my desk, in a fortnight. Here, I cannot refrain from remarking that I did not like Mr Wright. A clever, able man, he regarded his staff as creatures of a lower order and spent much of his time ingratiating himself with the upper crust of Downpatrick society and members of the local gentry. I was not accustomed to consider myself socially inferior to any bank manager and it has been a life-long regret that I never had a chance to say to him "I did not, Mr Know-all Wright, return to my desk in a fortnight, in fact, I did not see your blasted branch for twenty-five years and, by that time, I was married to a medical doctor and was, myself, an Honours Graduate of TCD" (a nice piece of venom to have been harbouring all these years!) I am grateful to two of my colleagues, Mr McCurdy, the cashier and Alex Gilmour, the senior accountant, for their more understanding farewells.

So, I left the Branch and made my way, on that lovely sunny morning, to my digs in Denver's Hotel. There my landlady Mrs Hayes was most sympathetic and wished me a safe return. When, a few days later my parents called to collect my belongings, Mrs Hayes, with tears which touched my mother's heart, declared that she would light a candle for me in the chapel and would pray for my safety.

On the journey home the very egotistical thought came to my mind, "The people on this bus don't realise that they are travelling with a young man on a special mission, a young man who has been called to the Colours!" But such ideas were quickly forgotten when I reached Belfast. I recall vividly the atmosphere then prevailing in the city.

I arrived in Donegall Place at the very moment when the heavy vehicles of a searchlight regiment, returning to base from a cancelled summer camp, were slowly and laboriously making their way along that thoroughfare. All work in offices and shops had stopped, and every window was filled with sombre faced

JOINING UP

spectators, young and old; and no-one cheered. That was what struck me most, the silence, the solemnity of it all. No-one wanted war. Everyone seemed to realise the awesome significance of what was happening; everyone looked with sober respect at the young men there, in trucks or armoured vehicles. I knew that never again would there be such a day in my life and so, sentimentally, I thought that I should in some way especially mark it. And so I did by purchasing, in Sharman Neill's, small silvery Celtic pins for Grannie and for my mother.

When I reached Tir-na-nÒg, I found my parents and grandmother behaving very bravely. Indeed, my mother was in a state of annoyance because the regiment's office kept phoning to enquire why the Knights had not yet appeared and that she had informed them that her sons had no notion of running away and would report, together, when the elder arrived from the country.

Jack and I then dressed ourselves in our denim overalls and caps, and together walked down Castle Park with a lump in each throat, and anguish in the hearts of those who saw us go.

But anti-climax quickly softened the blow. There was no accommodation at Dunmore Park to house a thousand men and so, having checked-in we were given the order to return to our home and to report again the following morning.

So the situation remained for about four days until A and B Sections of 21 Battery were ordered to take up gun positions near Greencastle and to occupy billets in the Old Star of the Sea Primary School. Jack's Battery, the 23rd, was at this time moved to the Kinnegar, Holywood, Co Down, so that the protection on both sides of Belfast Lough was in the capable hands of two Knight brothers.

Incidents of that first day's active service remain fairly vividly in my memory. Feverishly we dug gun-pits and filled sandbags in anticipation of the arrival of the battery's guns: this activity was a bore to the lads who were labouring men but for those used to sedentary jobs it was a purposeful activity. In the evening it was my task to supervise the serving of the first army meal. It

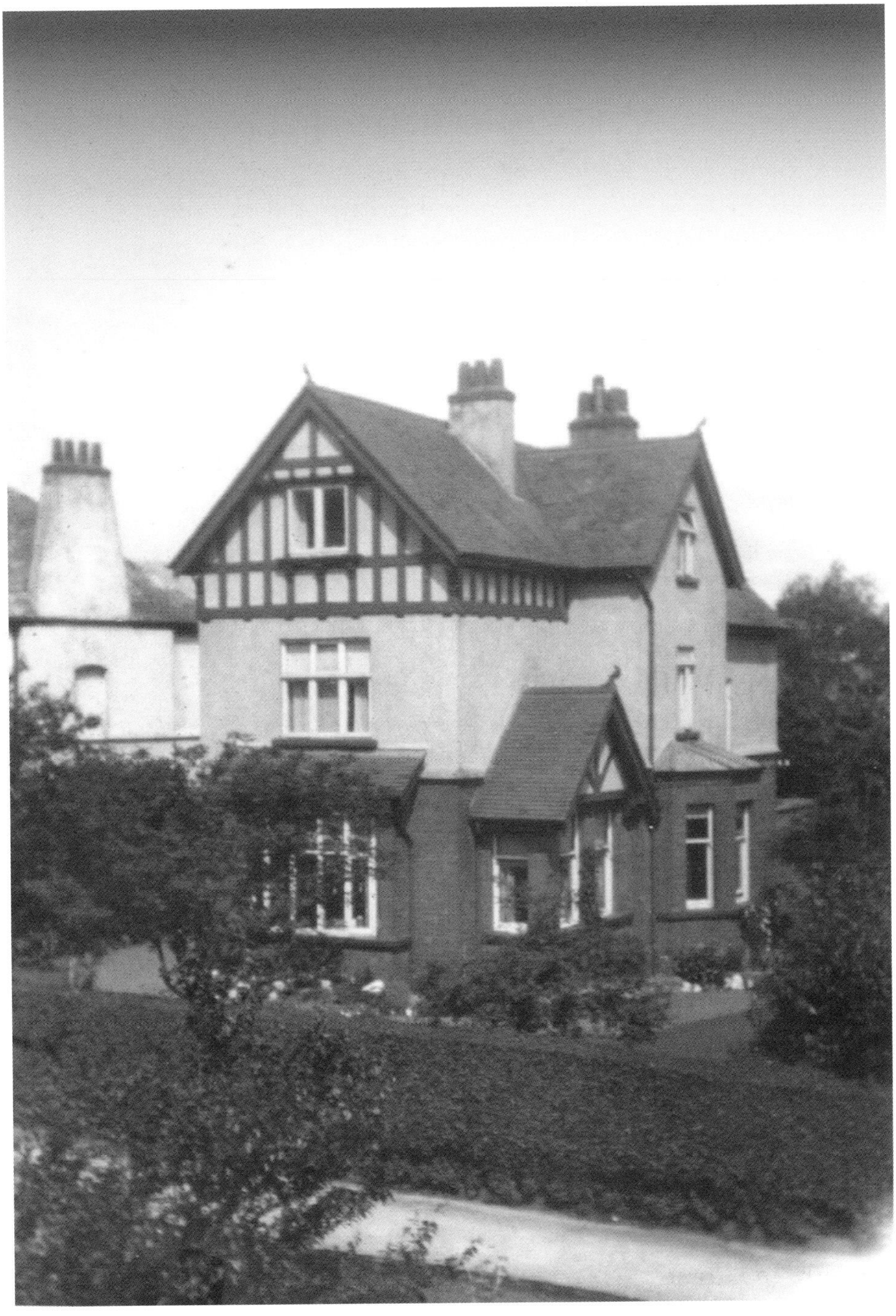

consisted of Sealord salmon, bread, margarine and tea. We possessed no culinary implements so I opened the salmon tins with a chisel and used that tool for dishing out each man's portion. The chisel also provided a means for breaking up the loaves. These uncouth conditions were accepted by the men from better homes but those from poorer backgrounds were much more critical. I think the well-to-do found such proceedings unusual and therefore interesting. Gunner Roy Preston (after the war a welfare officer whom my wife Helen knew) greatly resented his fate and lack of home cooking and would moan, "Oh, if my poor mother could see me now."

At night we were required to mount guard on the billets and on the gun-site. Again, for most of us this was something novel; few had been awake and wandering about in the first moments of dawn, but for the PSIs it must have been very tedious; they had to explain to us even the details of "two on and four off" and the challenge and responses of the sentries.

I had the misfortune to be the NCO i/c the guard at the first visit to the gun-site of our battery commander, Major Robin Forbes, a veteran of WWI. Prior to his arrival, Sergeant Leydon, a staff instructor, was rushed to us from RHQ with five rifles, and hastily instructed me and my four gunners in the drill for "Slope arms" and "Present arms", two movements that would be necessary to accord the major the correct salute as he appeared at the guard tent. Here, I have to record, that even in those days IRA attacks on armouries were not unknown and as we were considered inexperienced in the protection of weapons, it was decided that the rifles should be stacked around the pole of our bell-tent and secured by chain and padlock; the guard-commander being entrusted to keep the key in a safe hiding place.

Naturally we were keyed-up for this important occasion. In the guard-tent, gas masks strapped on our chests, steel helmets on our heads, we sat poised and ready to make a smart and soldierly appearance that would redound to the credit of our

PREVIOUS AGE:

Tir na n'Og,
5 Castle Park Belfast.
Irwin's parents' home.

troop and section. At last the major's car was seen approaching; the sentry shouted the traditional order "Turn Out, the Guard!", and at that critical moment I lost the key to the padlocked rifles. Desperately the sentry repeated his command; slowly the major drew nearer; still the sentry hollered, but all to no avail, for inside the tent every action was concentrated on frantic effort to find the missing key. Then one gunner, more ingenious that the rest, suggested that by lowering the tent pole we would be able to slip the rifles from beneath the encircling chain. This notion being immediately acted upon, the weapons were soon in our hands, but we still had to raise the pole and emerge into the open. This, at last, we accomplished, some vaulting through the door, others crawling under the wall-flaps, all half strangled in webbing equipment and all with helmets sadly awry. Practically breathless, I gave the order, "Guard, Present Arms." but the major, a choleric man at the best of times, put a curt end to the ceremonious compliments by assuring us, and me in particular, that never in his whole army career had it been granted to him to witness such a shambles. Our ignominy was completed when, on the major's departure, our troop commander lieutenant (fortunately for him recalled as an expert on tank construction at Harland & Wolff) having assembled the entire personnel of sections A & B, made this pronouncement: "The antics of Bombardier Knight and his Guard can only have been exceeded by the most flagrant follies of Fred Karno's Army!"[2]

Someone who had observed our performance told me that the tent's slow collapse and its internal heavings, caused by the rise and fall of our backsides as we reached for the rifles, conjured up in his imagination the picture of the death throes of a dinosaur or other antediluvian monster. It took some time to recover from the shame of this episode.

Then came 3 September 1939.

---

2   Any chaotic situation. Fred Karno was a late 19th century slapstick comedian

3 SEPTEMBER 1939

On that day, forty years ago, World War II began for the British people, and for the 8th Heavy Anti-Aircraft Regt (SR) RA.

My friends of B Section, 21st Battery, were in bell tents at the new primary school at Greencastle, Belfast, holding that strategic point from Hitler. We had so little knowledge of guns or gunnery that we did not know how to line up a gun through the muzzle rather than through the breech. The result of this ignorance was that in order to line-up a gun which was on a higher level than the predictor, we spent days digging a huge pit that would allow the gun barrel to be seen through from the Command Post.

However, the memorable moment of that day came when we were all lying in the tents sheltering from an incessant downpour that beat upon the canvas. Then it was that 2nd Lt. Harry McKibben ran down the lines and shouted in to each group, "The balloon's gone up!", in other words, war has been declared. This news I think the officers had received on the wireless.

As I try to recall my reactions, after so many years, I believe that they ran on these lines. First, a sick and sinking feeling in the stomach; secondly a fervent prayer that if the occasion arose that I should behave with a modicum of courage; and thirdly, I remember still being very aware of the distinctive smell of new canvas as it became warm and wet in the autumn rain.

The actual declaration of war did nothing to change the rhythm of the life which had been ours during the preceding week. No German fleet made its appearance in the lough and no bombers approached Belfast. We continued to spend off-duty hours at home, making our way by Gray's Lane to the Antrim Road but returning each night to billets. During those days we began to build up a relationship with the gunners that was to give us great pleasure while we served with the 8th and which was to last long after our return to civil life. Never before had I lived in such close proximity with what some would call the working class, and through the example of William John and by his influence, I found it to be an experience with amusement and interest. Strange facets of life were unfolded to me.

We slept in blankets, on the hard floor of the Star of the Sea classroom. My nearest companion was Gunner McKeown, a man remarkable for never having cut his toe-nails; this practice allowed his nails to curl down over the toes rather like the talons of an eagle. Not far away lay Gunner William Pollock, an overseer in Ewart's Mill, aged about forty-five but looking more like sixty. He explained to me that he found it necessary to wake three times in the night to smoke a Woodbine; if by mischance he ran short of these cigarettes he just removed some from beneath the pillow of his youngest child who, at the age of six, was already fond of a draw. On pay-nights the drunks would return in powerful form. They had to be gently persuaded to quiet down but often, when peace seemed to have been established and lights were out, a well-aimed boot hurled across the room to hit or fall upon some somnolent toper, would create fresh and prolonged uproar. You can imagine that in Castle Park I had not seen such sights as these. The regular NCOs, accustomed to instant obedience from those under their command, found it hard to adjust to the indiscipline of these soldiers of two-weeks' service. It was difficult too for these regulars to come to terms with rookies who, in many cases, were much better educated than they were themselves; for example, in the ranks, at that time, were to be found solicitors, engineers, teachers, bank clerks, business managers, accountants and civil servants. It spoke well for both sides that very quickly a feeling of mutual respect and affection was established.

These early days of war revealed to me the pleasure of an outdoor life. During five years I had been cooped up within the four walls of an office and many had been the days when I had looked out into a sunlit street and wondered why I had to be where I was. Now, each morning, I found myself out in the clean, clear air while the dew twinkled on the grass and, with no walls to confine me, could see far down the Lough or away to the Hills of Antrim. The smell of the up-turned soil in the gun-pits, even the physical exertion of digging or shovelling earth lifted the

JOINING UP

heart of one who, like Charles Lamb, had been 'long in office pent'. To add to this satisfaction was the enjoyment of wealth! In the Bank, my gross pay had been £2.10.0 per week out of which I had to pay £1.10.0 for 'digs', 10 shillings for various bank charges (widows' fund, guarantee fund) leaving me with ten shillings per week to provide for new clothes, travel fare home, toothpaste and tobacco – and entertainment. As an artillery sergeant my weekly pay came to £2.2.0 all found, with free tobacco – I hardly knew how to handle such riches. Indeed, I allocated £1 per week to a savings account and lived like a lord on the rest. Those savings provided the nucleus of my fortune when, at the end of the war, I decided to pay for my university education.

Before I forget, I must mention that on several occasions I was in charge of the RHQ guard at the Bishop's Palace, Antrim Road, about half a mile from home. There I remember being somewhat shocked to find that Gunner McKeown (for me he was an original) was eating his supper of fairly liquid Irish stew with the aid of a knife and a hunk of bread. I inquired if he had already lost the recent issue of cutlery, knife, fork and spoon. He replied that he still had these items in his kitbag but that he had never in his life made use of a spoon or a fork. Which reminds me that Gunner Charlie Robinson, a newspaper boy by profession, could only write letters on the floor because, in his home, there had never been a table, the furniture consisting of orange boxes. Poor Charlie was killed in the raid on our London gun-site. In the long watches of the night I found that men tend to become confidential and to reveal unexpected sides to their natures. This thought reminds me of another Gunner, one of the ugliest men I have ever met, and how, on some such guard duty he proudly showed me a grubby photograph of his youngest offspring and sought my opinion of the child's looks. It was a difficult moment; but I assured him that the lad was the image of his father. This verdict was received with pleasure.

As the weeks slipped on and the regiment acquired more and more equipment, it was announced that an advance party would soon be despatched to England, and that in a few weeks the rest of the men would follow to receive further training. Jeff and I, as 'instrument numbers' (i.e. we worked on predictors), were detailed for the advance party. I think we must have departed about the beginning of November and we were, fairly certainly, the first contingent of volunteers to leave the province. Led by a band, about two hundred officers and men marched out of Dunmore Park on a misty, murky evening and proceeded down Alexandra Park Avenue to the Shore Road and the Midland Station. I recall saying to myself, "This is it. This is how it must have been in the Great War for the men of the 36th Ulster Division. This is how they marched away; and how few returned." I was resentful too that there were no crowds to see us off. No one seemed to care.

At the station, however, such thoughts were quickly forgotten. News having leaked out that we were going away, the friends and relations of many of the lads turned up to bid them goodbye and wish them well. The farewell was boisterous! No sooner had we reached the Midland and fallen out than most were grabbed by hordes of their pals and rushed into the neighbouring pubs. A hardcore of sober, more responsible men remained on the platform to await in patience the arrival of the boat-train. As this train was long in coming, worried officers began to fear that the revellers would be too intoxicated ever to return, and so Jeff and I, with other sergeants, made hurried sorties to the pubs and there coaxed, cajoled and wheedled until we had all safe again within the platform's limits. Blackout had not yet descended on the city and so the picture that remains in my memory is the bright street lamps, the surging crowd, the range of gaily coloured bottles on shelves, the yellow glare of the brightly lighted bars, the shouts and cries of soldiery and well-wishers. All this was startlingly strange and new to me. I had never before been inside a Belfast pub, indeed, I had been taught to hurry by them as centres of sin and degradation, and here, in the space of half an hour, I had been in five or six, conducting out of them men old enough to be my father, married men, fathers of families, guilty of propelling them away from loved ones to a destiny that no one could foresee.

Eventually the advance party reached Aldershot and Blackdown but not before observing a fine example of the democratic principle for which we were fighting. This occurred on the station platform at Stranraer when our senior NCO, Sgt. Holloway, an artilleryman with fourteen years' service, a voice like a chain-saw, a square jaw and bulging eyes, forbade anyone to enter the train until he had selected the most comfortable compartment in which the sergeants would travel on that long, cold journey south. That job done, he addressed the men with the time-honoured order, "Get fell-in. Facing the boat. Pick up yer parrots and monkeys, and board the train." When all were safely entrained, with considerable complacency at his own cleverness, he joined the rest of us in the sergeants' compartment; the train rolled out of the station and he pulled on the strap to shut the window, but found that the window was without glass. We did the four or five hundred mile journey with an icy gale whirling around us; and all the while, Sergeant Holloway, grinding his teeth in fury, vowed vengeance on certain "f...ing bastards", never really identified.

It was odd to find oneself in and part of Aldershot, a place-name previously vaguely associated by us with the rough soldiery we had often seen in Clifton Street or taking some lass a-courting up the Cave Hill. Jeff and I, as sergeants, were placed in charge of one of the long sleeping huts, 'spiders' I think they called them. In my innocence, on arrival, I searched my locker for three 'army biscuits' which I assumed was some sort of iron ration but which turned out to be the standard army mattress, divided into three sections. Most of my memories of that dormitory centre on Jeff's and my attempts to stop fights and to extinguish the lights. We had a hilarious episode with Gunner Dawson whose exceedingly thin and exceedingly long frame and a mop of wire-like black hair earned him the nickname 'the

Piasaba brush³'. One night, arriving back in barracks just about blotto, he made several attempts to undress and to lay out his bed, but with no success. Then Jeff and I, to the great delight of his mates, decided to 'help' him. Somehow, we managed to remove his clothes but when it came to putting him to bed we were in difficulties. He was so tall and slim that he kept slipping through our arms, as slippery it seemed as an eel, and when we laid him on his mattresses one of them gave way and while his head remained on the pillow the rest of him remained on the floor beneath. This manoeuvre was attempted many times, and in the end it took six good men to place him safely in his couch.

It was at Blackdown that Jeff, on a bitterly cold night, did duty as orderly sergeant and encountered one of the great gentlemen of the regiment, Captain Workman MC, a First War veteran. The Captain, distressed by the freezing conditions, kindly gave Jeff the order, "Get the men something hot, Sergeant Jefferson, something very hot." But Jeff confided to me that in all the barracks, at that time of night, there were no facilities to provide even a cup of cocoa; still, we always gave Capt. Workman full marks for the thought.

Near Aldershot was a spot called Frimley Green and it was in this place that Sergeant 'Father' James Brown[4] (in civil life a director and South American sales representative for the linen firm of Jas. T Henry Ltd) first won his enduring niche in our affections. We four, Frank Reid, Jeff, 'Brownie' and I, one Saturday night, directed our steps to the local dance hall, but to Brown's way of thinking the occasion was lacking in excitement and character. This situation he quickly decided to alter by performing, to a somewhat bemused English audience, his excellent version of the Cossack clog-dance. This act being complete, from somewhere he produced a bicycle and again to

---

3   Piasaba: a South American plant, the fibres of which are used to make brushes, including brushes to clean gun barrels.
4   Father Brown: a fictional character in GK Chesterton's novels, solves detective mysteries.

the amazement of the spectators, insisted on riding it, many times, round the dance floor, backwards. That was a wonderful night!

Aldershot and Blackdown: there some instruction was given on the AA instruments, but of our time there I can only recall long rows of huts, a sergeants' mess in which you felt an interloper, long queues of men waiting for meals, squads marching hither and thither, officers of all ranks and uniforms to salute around every corner and a general sense of not-belonging.

The next step in our military education was our sojourn at the Firing Camp at Bude, Cornwall. There, in November, for the first two weeks we occupied tents on the edge of a high, windswept sea-cliff.

It was a healthy but chilling spot. The powers that be had ordered that, before breakfast, the men should do PT and take part in a mile run. Now, in November, darkness reigns still at 7.00am and it was something of a job to ascertain if every man was on parade; they had a habit of disappearing into the gloom. They had one other ruse worthy of recall; when we, sergeants, went down the lines enthusiastically shouting, "wakey wakey – on parade for PT", the more conscientious souls would tumble out, but they had wily friends who thought differently. These rascals, hearing our shouts, jumped from their blankets and, in a flash, attaching themselves like limpets to the top of the tent pole, hung there in the darkness and hoped that as bed places were empty, they would remain undetected until the PT parade was far away in the morning's murky mist. I must set this thought down, it is one that came often to me in army days: "men are always boys, they never grow up." Many years later, at TCD, I came across Sidney's lovely words, "So it is in men most of which are childish in the best of things, till they be cradled in their graves". Certainly these wonderful men from the Shankill and north Belfast, who in 21st Battery we came to love, remained, so far as I could see, boys at heart.

Our tented homes sheltered us for about a fortnight, but then the rain descended, and the floods came, and the winds blew, and beat upon that house; and it fell: and great was the fall of it. And the result was a chaotic quagmire, sprinkled with snow. As the gale howled above and the water flooded the ground, we heard on the wireless a spokesman for the War Office state that now no British troops were under canvas! After one hectic night when the camp was really devastated we were moved into commandeered hotels and guest houses in Bude, and not before time, we thought. When I think of what men endured on the Russian Front, I confess to being rather ashamed to have mentioned this minute discomfort.

The hours spent at the Firing Park blur into one long session of frustration, boredom, discomfort and humiliation. Each day we marched to the gun positions and there hung around in the bitter cold waiting our turn to fire the scheduled programme. There were endless hitches. The target-pulling-plane could not fly; if it did fly the sleeve would not open; required meteorological data could not be obtained; electrical faults developed in the cables, and so it went on and on. Then it must be remembered that we were, officers and men, a collection of amateurs or rookies and we were badgered, harassed and haunted by swarms of IGs (Instructors in Gunnery) and Ack IGs [sic](Assistant Instructors in Gunnery), each and all obnoxious know-alls, or so they seemed to us. "Aiming-Point, Tintagel Head..." words forever etched in my memory.

Yet there were good times too. We were delighted to learn that when the staid inhabitants of Bude heard that an Irish regiment had been stationed upon them they had asked for extra police protection. This gave us a reputation to live up to. In point of fact, the regiment, in deference to this request, appointed a piquet (a sergeant, a bombardier and six men) armed with pick shafts to patrol the town to control unruly members. I remember feeling very important as I paced sternly through the town in charge of this fine body of men; three months previously I had been behind a bank counter, now I was a guardian of the peace, vested with all the authority of a Gun-Sergeant of the British Army.

I would often meet with Jack in those days and it was good to have him so near. Sometimes we, with Jeff, Brownie and Charlie, would go to a little café, The Old Mill, a typical old English thatched building, and there gorge ourselves on blackberry pie and Devonshire cream. Seldom since has food tasted so good.

FRANCE 21 DECEMBER 1939

Once the Firing Camp training had been completed it was not long before we learned that we were bound for France to join the British Expeditionary Force (BEF). I do not recollect if we were granted embarkation leave but I know that we crossed from Southampton to Le Havre, arriving at that port on 21 December 1939. There was perhaps a political motive behind this move; the Unionist government may have wished to be able to report that, though conscription did not apply in Northern Ireland, the province had already a complete volunteer brigade serving in France, true to the tradition of the famous Ulster Volunteers and the 36th (Ulster) Division of the 1914-18 war.

One of my friends had joined with the rest of us as a territorial and, eager for promotion, had elected to work in the Battery office rather than with the guns and instruments. When war was declared he became isolated from his friends and, for example, had no chance to take part in the firing practices; instead he worked long hours on administrative matters. Perhaps that was the cause of his illness or perhaps it was some other mental strain, I cannot say, but it first came to notice at Blackdown Station when, as all boarded the train for Southampton, he just stood and stared at the carriages and made no move. Someone bundled him into a compartment and we heard no more of him until, half-way across the Channel, a gunner came to Jeff and me to tell us that our pal was acting very strangely. When we went along to see him, he stared at us uncomprehendingly; he did not know us. We were astonished but could do nothing but leave him in the care of a medical orderly, and that was the last we saw of him for close on two years. He was discharged from the army as medically unfit, a really heart-breaking case.

Having landed in Le Havre, our first billet was the spot where we disembarked, the Gare Maritime. In the huge, high-roofed hall of that station, we threw our two blankets on the ice-cold marble floor and tried to obtain some shelter from the chilling draughts. The worst frost for thirty years was gripping France and in that station we certainly felt it.

Men's tempers, already irked by the cold, were not mollified by orders which confined everyone to barracks, but perhaps this grumbling discontent persuaded the colonel, as it was so near Christmas, to relax the rule and to permit a visit to the city.

This first sallying-forth of the 8th Regiment into the city of Le Havre, and in particular, into its red-light district, the *rue des Galions* was something of an event, and the return to billets was on the same level. The lads quickly reached cafés and there, finding that cognac was cheaper than the Guinness they were accustomed to drink at home, consumed the stronger beverage in the same quantities. The results were disastrous. Men were soon 'out on their feet' or else ready to fight or brawl on the slightest pretext. Tragedy struck a neighbouring pioneer unit when two of their men, gloriously drunk, in making their way back through the ill-lit dockland, walked off a quay and were drowned. I remember that some of our men were so obstreperous when they reached the Gare Maritime, that the Regimental Sergeant Major, a giant of a man, was forced to knock-out the worst offenders. As you can imagine, the sight of men being so treated was, to me, most unusual.

Jeff, 'Brownie', Sergeant Holloway (our regular sergeant) and I celebrated that Christmas in our own way. One of Jeff's aunts had sent him a cold roasted chicken and this we took to a small patisserie which we had found on the ' Hormandie ' [rue Honnegar?], and the good people of the house agreed to make this bird the main course of the meal. The four of us gathered in a little alcove of the café and enjoyed some very good food. Sergeant Holloway, who must have found it hard to associate with sergeants of three months total army service, seemed scared that we would misbehave and so let down the traditions of the Royal Regiment. But we did not!

Very soon we were moved from Gare Maritime to Parc la Hève, a pre-war holiday camp, situated on the cliffs overlooking the 'roads', near the suburb of Sainte-Adresse. (One of the impressionists[5] has a painting of the area and its fashionable villas, in happier times). At Parc la Hève we first put our guns into action on French soil; and there we had time to learn something about them. But the dominating memory of those days is of the intense cold. At the gun-site, the wind howling in across the open sea cut like a knife. The ground was bound in an iron frost; every blade of grass, every twig and branch was enclosed in a deep layer of ice like the cut-glass crystals of a candelabra; our hot cocoa became frozen in what seemed a matter of seconds. Such conditions were very novel to men, like many of us, whose lives had been spent indoors. Yet there was something exhilarating about it all, to face into the north wind, and see, stretching far, far away, the blue of the sea beneath a bright cold sun; and to know that one was part of the English army in France, like Henry V at Harfleur and Agincourt, was a wonderful experience.

Our billets in the holiday camp were also very cold. The pipes having burst, the floors of the sleeping quarters were covered in ice. An abiding memory is of Brownie, Stanfield, Jeff and me all huddled into our four-berth bed, each of us fully dressed, plus pyjamas and balaclavas, and Jeff with a pair of warm woollen gloves, and the floor like a skating rink.

Some French soldiers shared the camp with us and we learned to look on them with compassion. Their uniforms were of the poorest material; puttees about as thick as a linen bandage; heavy, hob-nailed, coarse boots worn without socks. Maybe all of them were peasants, certainly they needed to come of hardy stock to endure the life imposed upon them. Then, too, they were

---

5 Claude Monet

miserably paid, a franc per day. In comparison we were wealthy. Later, we found ourselves in the same situation vis-à-vis the Americans. There is a heartlessness, maybe they call it realism, about the French, which I don't think one sees among the English, and some Irish.

We used to treat ourselves in a nearby café to *des oeufs et des pommes de terre frites*. They were served with a hunk of fresh French bread, butter and *café au lait*, all for five francs – about sixpence. Such luxury was far beyond the reach of the French soldier.

On off-duty hours Brownie, who was a great walker, would set out with me to tramp to Le Havre to explore its shops and showplaces. He was older and wiser than I was; he was a great companion. Jeff, Frank Reid and Sergeant Fred Green were less energetic, they found a small, comfortable hotel and there sipped their wines and played darts. The war seemed very far away. Most of the French army was on the Maginot Line and those at home regarded us as supernumeraries. Every now and again, a German plane dropped propaganda leaflets suggesting very clearly that while the French were in the front-line fighting, their British allies were in bed with the French wives. Which thought reminds me that our lads from the Shankill believed all French women to be of the same type as the Montmartre can-can dancers; this despite the fact that middle-class French women were far more rigidly moral than their counterparts in England. I used to be ashamed of the soldiers as, driving along in fatigue-lorries, they would shout 'Jiggy-jig, jiggy-jig' to respectable ladies, like my own dear mother, going about their everyday shopping in quiet streets or suburbs.

The brothels, or as the 8th Regiment preferred to call them, the broghils, continued to be a powerful attraction. The boys would regale us with what went on in these establishments – I remember that one girl was supposed to have accommodated twenty-one of our section in the one night – and invited us to do a tour of inspection. For long I steadfastly refused any such invitations for I was extremely frightened that if once I went there

I should be seduced by the allure of these ladies. At last however, having solemnly sworn Jeff and Brownie forcibly to restrain me if I ever showed an inclination for such amorous adventures, I consented to go. My fears for myself were groundless. On entering the first of these dens, *Le Chat Noir*, the immediate sight that met my eyes was of a fourteen-stone female, dressed in the briefest of grass skirts and nothing else sitting on top of a piano and leaving nothing whatsoever to the imagination. Far from being attracted, I was nauseated. It was a revolting scene. We visited one other equally sordid place, and that was enough. I've often wondered what was the ultimate fate of these women whose destiny was to satisfy the lusts of the toughest of seamen and the licentious soldiery. It is terrible to think that the creation of life can sink to such depths yet so it has always been – 'the oldest profession'. So far as I could observe, the men who made use of these women had no sense of guilt. It was all part of war and of life.

Sometimes I'd call to see Jack whose troop occupied a position on the Le Havre Promenade, at the Casino.

These days and nights had a great intensity for me. I was a soldier (of sorts) in France, following in the footsteps of generations of my countrymen. The shop signs, street names, because they were in French, acquired a strange attraction, even the smells were glamorous – Gauloises cigarette smoke and spilt red wine. When I walked through the narrow streets from the port, with the top storeys of the houses on opposite sides nearly meeting to the centre, I saw in the *charcuteries* and the *boucheries* fierce-looking females who seemed worthy descendants of Madame Lafarge of *The Tale of Two Cities*. They were tough people, they lived out their lives in the roughest of environments, far, far away from the middle-class ambience of the Stormont Stores and Robinson & Cleavers.

One task that came my way in those early days was to act as a foreman in the docks of Le Havre. As a sergeant I was expected to supervise four gangs of French stevedores, on four cranes, as they unloaded the ships coming in with vehicles, guns and equipment from Britain, a pretty well impossible task: I was further supposed to ensure that two hundred British drivers, awaiting the off-loading of their lorries, did not smoke all day, as they stood in the cold and rain; all this on the orders of a little popinjay of an RE captain who, when he made his rare appearances on the quays, would rate me severely if he found anyone having a quiet draw on a cigarette. I'd like to meet that idiot, and tell him now exactly what I thought of his English public-school prefectorial manners.

The phoney war continued but eventually we moved nearer the front. The train journey was a nightmare; so cold was the carriage that my ear, resting against the window as I tried to sleep, became frozen to the glass. Still, better than the 1914-1918 transport in waggons: *8 hommes; 40 chevaux.*

Our destination was somewhere near Arras, a name rich in associations, where we took up gun positions outside the city, finding billets in nearby villages. This area, having been a no-man's land of WWI, bore many traces of that conflict. There were no isolated farm houses as in Ireland; these had been utterly destroyed by the bombardments and in the resettlement of the area after that war the government had rebuilt the farmhouses in village clusters. In consequence, the farmers went off early in the morning from the villages to their strips of land. I might add that few men were to be seen, most had been mobilised and the women-folk, with bonnets and moveable screens to protect them from the wind sweeping across the plains, spent much time weeding the crops. An interesting point was that adjoining every house was a hut, roughly constructed of duck-boards and sleepers, that had been the home of each family when they had returned in 1919/20 to re-establish the devastated fields. In one village, I remember talking to an older woman who told me that she had seen her father go to the Franco-Prussian war of 1870; her husband to *la guerre de quatorze-dixhuit*; and her son to the present war.

Still we had seen no fighting, not even a German plane. Somewhat incongruously, we actually organised an excursion to the Thiepval Ridge to see where some fearful battles had taken place; Thiepval was, of course, the place where on 1 July 1916 the Ulster Division had been cut to pieces. It was an expedition not to be forgotten. So fierce had been the fighting there and so much blood shed that the French government had declared the district *une zone rouge (*or *sacrée)* where no cultivation of the soil was ever to be permitted. However, the outbreak of WWII had seen the lifting of this ban and, for the first time for thirty years, the land had been ploughed. Frank Reid, who had been on the Somme, but fortunately was ill just before the 1 July attack, showed us the positions held by the Ulstermen. Nearby we visited the Newfoundlander Memorial, trenches and dug-outs maintained just as the men had left them. The Newfoundlanders, like the Ulstermen, suffered very severe casualties. The Ulster Memorial is a copy of Helen's Tower at Clandeboye in County Down.

In this Arras countryside, on 1 April 1940, the 8th Regiment celebrated its first anniversary. It was not a dazzlingly successful function. Rain made our lines a quagmire; the food, served in dixies was cold – I have memories of congealed gravy and tepid Irish stew – all swilled down with large quantities of thin French beer. I think that it was on this occasion that I thought Willie John was going to die. Having partaken of the regimental feast he, with Sergeant Hewitt and other stalwarts, repaired to the local *estaminet* and proceeded to 'go along the shelf or shelves'. This name Jeff gave to the risky practice of having a drink from every bottle, in succession, on the shelves behind the bar. Sometimes the manoeuvre was repeated! I am extremely glad to state that at that time my only beverages were Dubonnet and champagne, two fairly harmless potions, and that I found that I could not drink in great quantities. Fortunately, I have never really enjoyed the taste of alcohol, but only the state of exhilaration it produces. Anyway, Jeff, never famous for having a strong stomach, went along the shelves; and then returned to our porter's lodge billets in Tilloy-lès-Mofflaines; I don't know whether it was the drink, or the greasy stew, or the intense cold or all combined, but he was so violently ill that he could not clamber up to the attic bedroom and I was left to make him as comfortable as possible, on a blanket, on the kitchen floor, before a dying fire. I had never seen anyone look so ill, so green, with sweat pouring from his forehead and hair. I really wondered if he could survive. However, he did, and lived to 'go along the shelves' on many another merry meeting, though possibly with slightly more care.

The last few weeks of the phoney war brought glorious warm sunny weather; our being in France seemed rather like a prolonged stay in a holiday camp. Jeff reminded me recently of how, as we went by lorry each morning to the gun-position, we passed a statue with an upraised arm (maybe a *calvaire*, I don't remember), and how two of our lads, Charlie Robinson and Cowboy Crawford, formerly Belfast news-boys, would shout, "Soorry mister...all sould out"! Both were killed in the London blitz.

Other famous characters among those Shankill men were Drunken Dan MacBride who managed to obtain his army discharge by repeatedly peeing his bed; Gunner Rossbottom, in civil life a 'sticky-apple' vendor who, when we asked how he managed to converse with the French in his black-market cigarette deals, told us that the language gave him no bother he just spoke to them like this: "You vant to buy de cigarette? Velly cheep – I sell you five or tenny". Then we had a limber-gunner, Gilmore, a strong Orangeman, who, every time he saw a French nun would mutter "Another bloody cormorant. We'll have no luck on the gun today, something will break!"

But the honeymoon period was fast coming to an end; Hitler had other ideas as to how we should spend that summer.

⚜

THE RETREAT

10 MAY 1940

On this day the real war began. My troop was in position east of Arras, close to the village of Tilloy-lès-Mofflaines and, up to that date, we had neither seen nor heard from any German; indeed the front line lay many miles in advance and we had occupied our time by digging very comfortable dug-outs in the fine chalk beside the guns. I remember how in our excavations we had unearthed tins of bully-beef and bullets from WWI. The cordite in the bullets ignited at the touch of a match. Below our gun-pits lay a small WWI cemetery to which we sometimes paid a visit to read the names of the men and of their regiments; Gunner Murphy, who hailed from the Shankill Road and had a great admiration for 'the Rifles' and the infantry in general, was often forcefully reminded by his friends that most of the names on the gravestones were those of foot-soldiers, and he was advised to content himself with the less hazardous life of the artillery-man. Gunner Murphy was, I should say in passing, one of the characters of the section. The unfortunate man had a cleft palate and early in our army days had lost his dentures. In consequence, his speech was somewhat difficult to follow, especially when he was moved to express his wrath after consistent goading from his mates.

On the morning of the 10 May 1940, our detached attitude to the war came to an end. I remember waking early and being immediately aware of new sounds in our neighbourhood and of a new sense of anxiety. The cause of this changed atmosphere was not hard to discover. In the distance, black smoke from burning farms and villages rose into the bright clear air; high overhead squadrons of planes, obviously German, sped, unmolested, across the sky; and then, closer, one noticed the haze of white dust hanging over the road from the front, a dust cloud raised by the stream of refugees who topped the nearby crest, hurried down the road and disappeared from sight. It was a procession that lasted from dawn to dusk.

I do not think that we had a chance to engage any of the enemy planes from that gun-site, for, in no time at all, orders came that the battery was to take up positions south of Arras. This was my first experience of the confusion of war. For weeks we had enjoyed the security of our well-built gun-pit, command post and dug-outs, and each evening had marched back in routine fashion to our billets in the village and to glasses of *vin blanc* in the *estaminets*. To be ordered to pack up and to depart, at a moment's notice, had a devastating effect – one felt very strongly that things were not being properly arranged. That 10 May I lost the gold wrist-watch given to me by my parents as a twenty-first birthday present. It was beneath my pillow in the billets but, when the order came to man the guns, I rushed from the blankets, forgetting the watch. We never had a chance to return. I've often wondered which tough German soldier fell heir to that watch.

The move, despite the flurry, was somehow completed and the guns brought into action, and by that I mean that they were set up as best one could expect from a collection of amateurs whose sole experience of gun-fire consisted of the twenty or so rounds they had managed to fire in the training course at Cleeve Camp, Cornwall, when they had been under the guiding hand of IGs and Ack IGs who had harassed and cursed them during one miserable and confidence-destroying fortnight.

As we moved back I noticed, in the square of Arras, three Irish Guards establishing themselves with their Bren gun at a street corner. There would be no retreating for them, and my heart went out to them in admiration, sympathy and gratitude.

From this second site, I had my first close-up view of German planes. In the afternoon there suddenly appeared, flying low and in tight formation, some fifty or sixty Heinkel bombers. Like great black vultures, the Iron Cross clearly to be seen on the fuselages, the planes, slowly circling deliberately dropped their bombs in the very centre of the city. Flames and black smoke arose from the devastated area. For me it was a terrifying sight, terrifying because of its total strangeness. Remember my background: a quiet, North of Ireland middle-class bank clerk from Fivemiletown and Downpatrick who had never before seen more than one plane in the sky at a time, and whose knowledge of destruction was limited to a whin fire on Cave Hill.

The pitiful state of our military training and of our preparation for war is surely revealed by the following incident. When those German planes were bombing Arras, a job accomplished in perhaps three minutes, Willie Jefferson and I were not on duty at the guns; we were supposed to be resting. However, William John was determined to have a go against the Hun and so, with him, I ran to the quartermaster's tent, drew two rifles and two clips of ·303 ammunition. I should add that we had, at that time, only six rifles per fifty men and that our musketry training was based on the five rounds each of us had fired at targets on Divis Mountain. Well, Jeff and I emerged from the Q's tent, clumsily opened the breech of the rifle and as awkwardly inserted the bullet clips. Thus equipped we launched our first attack on Hitler's Reich, three volleys at the planes which were by then probably several miles out of range. One could weep to think of it.

Prior to this Jefferson-Knight counter-attack, I recall that one Messerschmitt flew fairly high across our gun-site spraying the location with its machine guns. I think the pilot must have looked down on us with disdain and had not bothered to aim with care. Still, I remember with great vividness how, as I realised what was happening, I hurled myself to the ground, trying to get under the cover of a daisy. The memory of the sight of those black planes sweeping in and bombing Arras remains with me still, as does the strange sensation I then felt that this was reality; I was not sitting in a Belfast cinema watching it.

The days that followed were again filled with complete confusion, a terrible baptism for the young officers who commanded us and who had no more experience than we had. Looking back, one sees that it was probably a political ploy to have some Ulstermen serving with the BEF at the earliest opportunity; and so, untrained and ill-equipped, the 8th Regiment, over one thousand officers and men, had found itself, on 20 December 1939, in *la douce France*. How very lucky, or rather how blessed by God they were not to be annihilated by the superbly led and trained German army and air force.

Another picture of those turbulent three weeks comes to my mind. For a short while our section was in a position near Hazebrouck; the guns sited on one side of a main road and the cookhouse and waggons on the other. Down that road, from early morning to late at night, the refugees passed. They travelled mainly on huge four-wheeled farm carts, the like of which I had never seen before. On the vehicles were piled the hastily collected household elements that, I suppose, the unfortunate people considered essential, tables, chairs, sewing machines, clocks, cupboards, blankets, mattresses, pots and pans. Perched in this agglomeration were the young children and, usually, on the top of the stack, an old crone, the great-grandmother, it seemed, of the family. But every means of transport had been pressed into use: hand carts; motorcars with several mattresses on the roof; vans and lorries, all loaded down with pathetic bundles of untidy luggage. Among the never-ending flow, I saw an old man wheeling his wife on the bar of his bicycle; another pushing his aged spouse and their few earthly possessions in a wheelbarrow; the fire-engine of some small village taking with it the families of the fireman; and then, most memorable of all, down the highway came two or three medium cannon, each drawn slowly, in tandem, by a couple of emaciated white farm-horses, by the side of which plodded the artillerymen in the traditional blue of the *poilu*, their coat-tails buttoned back to allow their legs more freedom to march. To me it seemed that these antiquated guns, horses and weary gunners could be the last remnant of the *Grande Armée*, struggling home in the great Napoleonic disaster, the terrible retreat from Moscow. Men and equipment belonged to another century, and once again I found it nearly incredible that I was there in the flesh, that what was before my eyes was not a picture on the screen or evoked by the descriptions in a historical novel.

At Hazebrouck, our Section, for the first time, encountered the problem of the breakdown of regular supplies; the ration-lorries were unable to find the rear food-dumps and, in consequence, quartermasters and cooks had to forage the area for what could be obtained. The result was that sometimes we had a surfeit of eggs, perhaps a dozen per man per meal, and certainly, somehow, gallons of Army rum came into our possession. This had nearly disastrous consequences, for the men filled their water-bottles with rum and drank it like tea. Under such circumstances, tempers flared and I remember how one Gunner McKeown, in civil life a coal-man's assistant, grabbing a hatchet in a mad frenzy, jumped clean through the petrol-cooker's flames in an attempt to wreak his vengeance on a cook who, he believed, had insulted him. So dangerously intoxicated was McKeown that we had to catch him, hurl him to the ground, tie him with ropes and finally hoist him thus pinioned into the rear of a truck. (We were supposed to be fighting the Germans!)

I think that it must have been at the Tilloy-lès-Mofflaines site that Jeff and Andy Shanks were sent off to halt the German tank break-through with the section's anti-tank rifle. With typical army efficiency the powers-that-be had seen fit to despatch Willie, who even then was extremely short-sighted, on a two day anti-tank rifle course – Jeff who, only a few months before, while driving the family motorcar on the Antrim Road, Chichester Park, had asked "Monk, is that a cow or a tram in front?" Anyway, it fell to his lot to set out, accompanied by only Andy, to find a spot from which he could fire on the Panzers. I will never forget the look on his face, first of astonishment at receiving such an order, and then the closing of his mouth and the jutting out of his chin as he set out to obey it. He was brave.

However, after a couple of hours, he returned and with this tale to tell. On reaching the crossroads to which he had been directed, he found there a regiment of heavy French tanks which had either retreated before the Germans or was waiting to engage them. When the French saw the anti-tank rifle (which fired a projectile of all of two ounces) they laughed heartily at Jeff and advised him to return with all speed, and no second thoughts, to his unit.

At the Hazebrouck site the refugees still came down the road. It was as if a whole countryside was in flight, the entire population of say, the North of Ireland, fleeing South and all passing along the same road.

It was at this site that we had our first gunner killed in action; a battery clerk, Gunner Baird, who had come from HQ with a message. Just as he arrived on the site a JU 88 dive-bomber, hedge-hopping across the fields, suddenly appeared to the left of the guns and in less time that it takes to write, had machine gunned the position and disappeared. The poor little clerk who had dived for cover beneath a lorry was hit on the head and died instantly.

Then, to our utter consternation, four medium German tanks appeared at a distance of some five hundred yards, debouching from a sunken lane way; these were, I suppose part of the spearhead of the great armoured drive that was scything its way through the French and British armies. It was not possible for us to range on the tanks because of a farmhouse, packed with refugees, that lay between. At this moment further news came through that we were to retreat; I am not sure of this, but retreat we did, in wild panic. I have always felt that there we missed our chance to win a VC and that all of us should have died by the guns. But we did not and maybe the fruits of our subsequent careers in some way compensated for the sacrifice we should then have made. Anyway, for me and for any like me, I cannot think of us having any right to wear with pride a Dunkirk medal. That unofficial decoration (concocted by some French civilians and Legion Associations after the war) should have been reserved for the real heroes of Dunkirk, the lads who held the perimeter, died at their posts and allowed the rest of us to escape.

THE RETREAT

Our return to France in 1944 did something to lessen the sense of shame that is attached to that retreat. I write here what I feel, all the while recognising that I am not of the stuff heroes are made and thankfully acknowledging how blessed I have been to have been permitted to enjoy such a happy and fairly useful life. It may be some excuse to add that we had not the training which might have instilled in us a confidence in ourselves and in our guns; we had never previously seen a tank, friendly or hostile, nor fired even a practice round against such a target. But this is only an excuse.

The retreat turned into a rout and we quickly learned that we were not the only group to have behaved with less than traditional courage. French, Belgian and British troops were heading, they knew not whither so long as the direction was away from the enemy.

Gradually it became known that all were making for the Channel ports. Jeff and I, with about thirty of our section, did the journey in a three-tonner driven by Albert McKibben; he had christened his truck Hetty in honour of his wife, and all night long as we motored on and on he would shout encouragement to the engine in the cry "Hack on, Hetty!". Again that memory is something of a nightmare.

We drove towards the coast in the dark, with dimmed lights, on roads congested with the debris of two or three armies. There were French convoys making towards the front; the remains of French divisions coming back; British convoys moving forward; others in retreat; disorganised units of the Belgian forces; a long motorised ambulance brigade trying to force its way through this unspeakable confusion and muddle. At one river bridge McKibben, finding his road blocked, turned on to the narrow foot-way, weaving through ornamental trees and shrubs to win a march on the other bewildered competitors. This may seem a trivial point to mention, but my motoring experience in the Knight family's Austin 12 was of such an orthodox nature that the action of wilfully mounting the footpath suggested that we were indeed in a dire situation.

There came a point when we could proceed no further in the three-tonner and so we joined the hordes plodding doggedly in a direction which, by silent consent, appeared to be the right one. The name flashes on shoulders revealed the extent of the disaster; small groups of apparently leaderless men from different regiments and corps shuffled along in a shabby medley. That night Jeff and I slept in a broken-down hen house, and sleep we did, for we were weary.

In the morning, for the first time I think in our comfortable middle-class lives, neither of us knew where our next meal was to come from, and that is an unpleasant realisation. Then it was that I, pushing down on a loose floor-board, discovered a large hunk of stale green-moulded loaf – doubtless part of a meal intended for the previous occupants of our shelter. We seized upon it, eyed it with distaste, but ate it lest worse befall!

28 MAY 1939: HMS MONTROSE

As the sun rose, we tramped on with the long mass of straggling fugitives at last reaching the canal tow-path that encircled that part of Dunkirk. Over the town hung a blanket of black smoke, the residue of the previous days' and nights' bombing. At so early an hour no German plane had deigned to visit us.

The beaches and dunes were eventually reached and Jeff, James Brown (Father Brown) and I settled ourselves to await our fate. I don't know what the others thought but I was sure that, if death spared us, we would be made prisoners of war; but death seemed the more likely option. The scene that lay before our eyes filled us with foreboding.

The beach was covered with abandoned lorries, burnt-out command-waggons, personal equipment and loot: barometers, clocks, wireless-sets, pictures, vases, a fireman's brass helmet, all the trumpery that men had gathered from the empty houses they had wandered through on their way to this stretch of sand. To save themselves and gain a place on one of the small boats, all such articles had to be dumped. Every now and again another truck would arrive, the driver dismount, toss some petrol on his vehicle and, in an instant, it was another blazing bonfire adding its quota of smoke, horror and destruction. Men roamed aimlessly through the wrecks or dug shallow pits in preparation for expected strafing and bombing attacks.

Jeff, Brownie and I sat together, and it must be confessed that we displayed little initiative. We had brought our small section to this spot and any further action seemed beyond us. We had no food, no tobacco, no sweet ration, and we just sat there. But not so our gunners! They, not having been blessed at home with comfort and security, had learned in the rough society of the side streets of Belfast to fend for themselves. So it was that, as we three sergeants sat staring into space, those lads, having explored the immediate neighbourhood, discovered an abandoned NAAFI and secured ample supplies of cigarettes, chocolate and sweets. I shall never forget how one, Gunner George Turkington, a reserve tram-conductor, came up to the three of us and from his bulging battledress blouse handed each a fifty tin of Wills cigarettes and numerous bars of milk chocolate.

Sometime during the morning, Jimmy Robinson came and sat near me. A shop assistant in Anderson & McAuley's and a member of St Nicholas Parish Church, Carrickfergus, he was one of the finest Christians I have ever known. In crowded barracks rooms or Nissen huts, each evening, Jimmy knelt beside his bed to say his prayers and men, seeing him thus engaged, so respected him that they would cease their talk and foolery and silence would reign until he had finished. They had come to know that if any dirty or unpleasant job needed to be done, Jimmy was always sure to be the first to volunteer. He was accompanied by his friend, Chris Calvert, a less dedicated spirit, who was inclined to believe that Jimmy 'volunteered' too much but, nevertheless, invariably followed his pal. Well, on that Dunkirk beach, Jimmy, firm in his Christian faith, was unruffled and serene. He asked me if I should like him to read to me from the Bible and I, I am ashamed to say, clutching at any straw, readily agreed. He then read from John's Gospel, Chap 14:

> Let not your heart be troubled: ye believe in God, believe also in me
> In my Father's house are many mansions; if it were not so, I would have told you.
> I go to prepare a place for you..."

Jimmy was one of the best men I ever met; the sort of character to whom one would unhesitatingly entrust one's life. After the war, he started in business for himself but he was too honest and too kindly to achieve success; he was robbed right, left and centre. He abandoned this venture and worked for the youth training centre in Lisburn.

If this good man sought to bring us spiritual comfort, help and hope of a more mundane nature came from the Royal Navy. Surrounded as I was by such sorry evidence of incompetence and epic disaster it is well-nigh impossible to express the extent of my admiration for the behaviour of the naval ratings who came ashore to hasten our embarkation from those sand hills of hopelessness. With chin-straps firmly holding their caps in position, wearing blue great-coats, short canvas gaiters and green webbing equipment, each with a rifle slung on the shoulder, they exuded an absolutely extraordinary air of confidence and efficiency. "The Navy's here – so all is well!", certainly some such thought was mine. One sailor, halting near our group, asked if we would like a lift in his lorry to the harbour where troops were being taken off. We all clambered eagerly aboard and then the lad in question announced:" This is the first time I've ever had a chance to drive one of these f...in waggons!" He was learning to drive on the beaches of Dunkirk.

At the harbour, we found a very long queue, four deep, slowly making its way down a narrow pier at the end of which lay the destroyer HMS *Montrose*. The movement towards the ship being nearly non-existent and some men at the rear beginning to attempt to surge forward, a young officer, with all the appearance of a Territorial, drew his revolver and declared that he would shoot the next man who stepped out of line. His action has always lingered in my mind; he was all alone, he was young, but he knew exactly what required to be said and done.

It was just at this moment that Jeff, Brownie and I made our self-sacrificing – and self-preserving – contribution to the Dunkirk story. An ambulance convoy arriving at the shore end of the pier unloaded the wounded and asked for volunteers to carry the stretchers down the long pier to the ship. No one seemed to be in any hurry to undertake this task and so Jeff and I lifted one while Father Brown, with someone else, took another. Slowly we edged our way up the pier passing the queue members on our way; after managing about one hundred yards of this transportation we halted, expecting others to volunteer for the job. But no one stepped forward. Then it was that I think all of us, at the same instant, recognised that we were onto a good thing for, without a doubt, by carrying the stretchers we had advanced closer to the destroyer in a few moments than we could have managed in perhaps three or four long hours. Immediately Jeff and I again took up our stretcher-case and, with Brownie now in front calling "Make way for the stretcher cases", we reached the head of the queue, carried our wounded on board ship, and by these proceedings probably saved ourselves from the later bombing and strafing of the pier.

When the *Montrose* (a name I shall never forget) had taken on her capacity load, we set sail for the open sea.[6] Jeff and I were asked to attend to the wounded who lay on the open deck. Jeff's particular charge was a grizzled haired, stockily built man, aged about fifty, who, covered by an army blanket, was suffering much pain. From time to time Willie would try to make him more comfortable and, patting him on the head, sought to encourage him by murmuring, "You'll be all right, old boy, we'll soon be there, mate." This somewhat familiar tone was seen to be rather out of place when, on this ship giving a roll, the blanket slipped from the wounded man's shoulder and he was revealed to us as a Brigadier! My charge was a young officer of the Green Howards.

---

6   28 May, *Montrose's* only crossing in the evacuation

He too was in a bad way. As the coast of Kent approached he overheard someone mention the white cliffs. I shall never forget his words to me: "Could you lift me up a bit so that I might see again the white chalk cliffs of England."

Our channel journey was not without incident. About halfway over, three or four German bombers spotted us and one, detaching itself from the others, flew directly across our path and let loose its load of bombs. We could see them coming five in a row, and of these, it seemed certain that the last must hit us. Yet, in what must have been the final split second the *Montrose,* taking violent evasive action, flicked her stern from under the bomb which, exploding so close under water, extinguished all the lights below deck. I recall that after that I loosened the laces of my boots. I should also mention that my geography being rather weak and my knowledge of the exact location of Dunkirk obscure, I could not be persuaded that we were crossing the Channel but rather that we were being taken to land on French soil somewhere further west. It was not to be believed that we were returning to England so soon; the real war had begun only three weeks previously.

At Dover there awaited us a welcome that I felt we little deserved. We were treated as heroes, and most of us were not. At the quayside, colonels, brigadiers, staff-officers, generals fell over themselves to reassure us, to comfort us and to speed us on our way. Our train was bound for Aldershot and the artillery camps on Salisbury plain. It was an unforgettable journey. Looking from the carriage window, as the train made its way up through the Kentish villages and the suburbs of London, I saw old gentlemen quietly engrossed in their game of bowls (shades of Drake!) in the municipal parks, and young people diverting themselves on tennis courts and cricket grounds, yet all of us on that train knew that only forty miles away, beneath a huge cloud of smoke, amid burning buildings and falling bombs, the English army, devoid of equipment, was struggling frantically to live and to escape. No one, at home, seemed to realise what was happening.

Still, that is not altogether true. At every station halt, women like our mothers waited to hand in tea, cakes and buns, and looks that spoke volumes of concern and compassion. Never before or since, of that I feel pretty sure, was spread abroad in England such a feeling of sympathy and friendliness. This was certainly one part of the Dunkirk spirit; the other manifested itself in a sort of dour realisation that the phoney war was over; that the country was in deadly peril; and that we were alone. The home-coming troops felt only the first part of that spirit.

And those troops were weary, very, very weary. I don't think that we had had proper food for about ten days, our hours of sleep had been few; and we had all the weariness of defeat. Imagine then what it was like, at Salisbury plain, to eat a well-cooked meal and then, with an armful of blankets, to tumble into a bed, at last, and fall asleep.

> Oh sleep it is a gentle thing,
> Beloved from pole to pole,
> To Mary Queen the praise be given,
> She sent the gentle sleep from Heaven
> That slid into my soul.

So said the Ancient Mariner, and though we were in no form for poetic quotation, his thoughts expressed our own. We slept non-stop, or nearly so, for thirty six hours; we could hardly bother to attend meals.

At last, however, we roused ourselves sufficiently to send telegrams of our safe arrival to Castle Park and Old Cavehill Road. We had no news of Jack or Charlie Jefferson. That duty exhausting our entire money supply, we had to await a time when the army would find some method of giving us an interim payment. Meanwhile we had nothing to do, except to visit Stonehenge, which stood at half a mile distance from our huts. We visited that monument, I seem to recall, at least twice every day.

Looking back to those three most hectic weeks of my life, I cannot help but wonder at the strange workings-out of Fate. We, for the most part untrained and ill-equipped, came home routed and dismayed, but we lived to see another day and, even later, to live lives perhaps useful to our generation. The Germans, who defeated us, were the military flower of Europe, superb specimens of young manhood, splendidly equipped, trained and imbued with a passionate conviction of the worth of their cause. The brilliance of their victories must have aroused in them a veritable rapture of success. Yet few of these magnificent young warriors can have survived the war; they must have, for the most part, fallen in Russia, the desert or the western front, the opportunity to return to the contentment of peace forever denied them. One can imagine that those severely wounded in the 1940 campaign may have thought their sufferings worthwhile but surely, in the utter defeat of 1945, their bitterness must have been extreme. At least, we were spared that.

1940 Leave after Dunkirk. With his Grandmother

THE RETREAT

In 1990 Irwin Knight gave some further details of his time at Dunkirk, answering questions from a great-nephew who was writing a school project.

During the retreat his group was in the middle, *but the speed of the German advance was so swift that soon their tanks were uncomfortably close.*

When we arrived at the beaches we were very tired and so we settled ourselves in the sand-dunes and attempted to scoop out "funk-holes" into which we could dive if the bombers attacked.

From the beginning of the retreat the food supplies became irregular and finally stopped. Once we camped beside a deserted farm and there we rounded up all the hens, killed them, boiled them in dixies and each man had a chicken to himself. Luxury! On another occasion we came across a cow that had a leg shattered by a bomb. I was deputed to shoot the poor animal. One of our gunners had been a butcher in civil life so he set about carving up the carcass. I forget if we ever had time for cooking.

On arrival in England we were welcomed by the wonderful ladies of the W.I. (Women's Institute) who gave us tea and cakes – indeed we were treated as heroes and we were definitely no heroes. We then boarded a train from Dover...

We eventually arrived at Salisbury or thereabouts, and there after a meal we lay down and slept and slept and slept. You can imagine that everything was pretty mixed up at our camp. There were men from, I think, every Royal Artillery regiment and from other formations. It took days to begin the sorting out and as we were a newly formed Irish Territorial outfit no one had ever heard of us and did not know where to send us.

After some weeks we set out in search of our own Regiment, a quest which took us to Cornwall, South Wales, London, North Wales and eventually Blackpool. Then we began, after a short leave home, to reform.

In my pleasantly unadventurous life the weeks of retreat are, I suspect, the most vividly etched in my memory. I regret that I have no heroic personal exploits to relate of that time; the real heroes were the lads who held the perimeter and allowed the rest of us to escape.

3 FROM DUNKIRK TO THE INVASION: 1940-1944

AUTUMN-WINTER 1940-41: COVENTRY, LONDON BLITZ, STOCKTON

There was a time, some thirty years ago, when I could have recorded, with a fair degree of accuracy, the sequence of events and movements which filled this period of my life. Now, I must confess to have retained of them only a rather jumbled memory. This is perhaps the more strange in that it was then that I took some of the most important decisions of my entire career; first, to become a commissioned officer and second, to resign from my job in the Northern Bank and to attempt, when the war ended, to obtain a university degree.[7] These steps did take me truly into a different way of living, intellectually and socially, which sounds most pompous but which I believe to be correct.

By becoming a commissioned officer, during war-time, I had an entry into the highest, or nearly highest, levels of society and this gave me an insight into a way of life of which, while I was outside it, I was envious, but which I learned to see as in many ways no different from that which I had always known; the same petty squabbles and snobberies and, it must be said, the same signs of goodness. However, there is a great gulf fixed between those who have never had to consider money or expense, and those for whom the acquisition of a wage or salary is the first consideration of existence. Yet I came to pity those to whom all material things had been given at the age of 18 or 20; it seemed

---

7   He was still posing this possibility to his sister in Spring 1943

FROM DUNKIRK TO THE INVASION: 1940-1944

to me that for such there was nothing left in life for which to strive; little satisfaction, for there was little to attain. Having mixed in this society I was not, after the war, easily impressed by the social pretensions of people who would have liked to have been thought superior; mingling in society gave me a social confidence which I lacked. Not many have dined with a future Captain of the Yeomen of the Guard.[8]

My success at the university sustained or increased this feeling of confidence. I would say to myself. "These people are all right, they rather fancy themselves intellectually, but I have a better degree than most of them". All this must make the reader think that I was and am a man of boundless self-confidence. Nothing could be further from the truth; the fact is that I seemed to require those crutches of self-esteem, and that none of my friends required any such support. I have always felt a sense of inferiority because of my lack of physical courage; I envy that of my brothers Jack and Lindsay. I suppose that is why I am inordinately proud of having served as a soldier, while remembering always that the real soldier is the infantry man, which I was not. That I did actually join-up gives me a sort of warm glow as I think of it. I commune with myself and mutter, "Well, once, at least, you had the courage to take a risk." Still, I must say again lest I be thought boastful, as regards courage and daring I have always felt much inferior to other men and women, and I hope this balances the earlier assertions of self-confidence.

However, to return to the chronicling of my army days. So far as I can remember the 8th Regiment re-formed in Blackpool, in the late autumn of 1940, and our first posting to gun-sites was to Coventry. In that city I came across, for the first time, a bitter anti-Irish feeling. This was not to be wondered at for, just prior to the outbreak of the war, the IRA had carried out a bombing

---

[8] Probably Michael Onslow, later 7th Earl of Onslow, captain of the Yeomen of the Guard 1951-60.

campaign there in which several civilians had been killed. I recall in a bus someone saying to me "You surely are not Irish – you have a kind face."

Coventry, at that time, was a boom town owing to the high wages being paid to the armament and aircraft workers. And, like most boom towns it was a fairly chancy place; in the pubs the soldiers would often find that a round of drinks had been sent to their table and paid for by an armament worker, male or female. While in Coventry I visited Geordie Scott, Eric's nephew, who was a pupil apprentice at the great electrical firm of British Thomson Houston, in Rugby. George showed me how to make toasted cheese on an electric radiator. We were generally feted in that area because we were known to have been at Dunkirk; we enjoyed an undeserved respect.

Hitler's determination to break the spirit of the British people by an all-out aerial attack on London caused our next move, for off to London we went and were there during the entire Blitz. I should add that by going to the metropolis we were spared the fearsome attack on Coventry,[9] the worst bombing in England up to that date.

In London, we established gun-sites at Gunnersbury Park, in South Ealing or Ealing Broadway, just off the Great Western Road, the exact details have slipped from my memory. At this position, my troop had one of its worst experiences of the war. In one particularly heavy raid, the Germans dropped a stick of bombs right across the gun-park, killing 'Cowboy' Crawford and Harry Robinson, two Belfast newsboys, and wounding several others. For Jeff and me the occasion was a near thing. During a lull in the firing, Jeff had wandered over from his gun-pit to the command post, a distance of ten yards, when we both heard the scream of a heavy bomb coming apparently down on top of the pair of us. Instinctively, we threw our arms around each other

---

9   They left Coventry three days before the raids started on Coventry, 14 November 1940.

and hurled ourselves to the ground awaiting the end, or the terrible explosion which must surely come. But it did not come and only in the morning, after the firing had ended, did we discover that the bomb had struck the corner of the gun-pit where Jeff was accustomed to shelter. There was a neat tunnel to be seen where it had entered the ground, but it had not exploded. Indeed, had it burst, the entire gun-team would have been wiped out.

I recall too the night 'Jerry' set the London docks ablaze. This gigantic fire was some fifteen miles away from us but its glow lightened the darkness of our position. In passing, I should say that the 3.7 shell-cartridge in brass which I had in the hall at Rosebank[10] came from some of the ammo fired by our troop at this time. I smuggled it home because I hoped that one day I should use it as a gong as Captain Moore had done with a similar brass case in Clonlea.[11]

It was an odd experience to live through the Blitz, and, to be truthful, the soldiers had the best of it. I pitied the firemen and police who were working right in the centre of the flaming target areas; and the unfortunate civilians who, having spent the night in air-raid shelters or under their stairs, had to face out to work in the morning. It was a pitiful sight to see the people, whole families, lying in the London Underground stations, trying to obtain some quiet and sleep. One walked over and around these groups when moving towards the trains. When an air raid was imminent a warning was flashed on the cinema screen and anyone wishing to leave the building was asked to do so at once. It was considered cowardly to allow Hitler so to interrupt one's entertainment and, as a soldier, I felt that I had better sit on, but I must say, in much fear and dread, with many an anxious glance at the huge concrete and steel girders just above my head. I did not enjoy these films.

---

10 His house at Banbridge
11 Captain Moore of the Merchant Marine lived in Clonlea on Glenburn Park, where Irwin lived as a child

Anti-aircraft command was always endeavouring to think of new ways in which to beat the bombers. The 8th Regt was employed in one such ruse. As Jerry nearly invariably followed the same path each night, in from the south-east coast and up the Thames to London, it was decided to position, in complete secrecy, a mass of guns which would hurl a devastating barrage against him. Thus it was that each evening, just as dusk fell, we hurried with our equipment to the Essex marshes and there the entire 24 guns of the regiment, placed in a great circle, were co-ordinated to deliver a sudden burst of AA fire. I never learned if we had much success; I believe that the first night's firing caused the enemy some dismay, but I certainly remember that we thought that we were really suffering. The marshes were water-logged, the mud squelched over the top of our Wellington boots. We had to stand – we dared not sit – and it was bitterly cold. It must have been, for we were served with a rum ration, my first experience of that chest-warming liquor.

I should add that the night on which Cowboy Crawford and his friend Robinson were killed, we, my section, were fortunate to be on duty at the guns. Had we not been so engaged, we would all probably have been killed or wounded for in the morning, returning to our tents, we found that fragments of the shrapnel had passed through the blankets and bedding where we would have been sleeping. Again, as at Coventry, we were generally well received by the locals. While at Ealing we were made honorary members of the local Tennis Club – tennis courts and gun-pits, cheek by jowl! It's strange how people adapt to conditions, but I suppose because death was so close, people lived more intensely in those days. Maybe it was just my provincial innocence that made me think so, but in the taverns there was always, at night, a feeling of excitement and gaiety, and kindliness that was a new experience for me. I suppose all young soldiers who were away from home for the first time think like this. As Kipling says:

> "And single men in barracks don't grow into plaster saints, but they don't become scoundrels either!"

FROM DUNKIRK TO THE INVASION: 1940-1944

We were in London all that winter and seemed always to be on duty. The blitz has been described by more able pens than mine and so I can only add my memory of the regular nightly wail of the air raid siren, followed nearly at once, by the peculiar 'up and down' drone of the German bombers, then began the vivid flashing of our guns, the scream of descending bombs, the lurid light of blazing buildings, the whistles of the air raid wardens and the ambulance sirens sounding. Then, at last, a grey dawn broke, no more bombers came, the all clear sounded, and one thanked God inwardly for having been allowed to survive another night. In those days we remained in the suburbs; it seemed folly to venture into the centre of London, into an area we did not know.

From London, as far as I can recall, the regiment moved to the north-east of England, to the Tyne and Tees, districts which were beginning to become Hitler's main target. The chief memories I have of that area are of the blast-furnaces stretching from Stockton to Grangemouth;[12] of the endless ugly slag heaps; of the huge mass of Dorman Long's steelworks, and of the bitter, bitter cold wind that blew in on those winter days from the North Sea. No wonder that the Geordies are tough, and, incidentally, I never met a bad Geordie.

SPRING 1941; COMMISSIONED OFFICER: WALES, GOUROCK

It was from Grangemouth gun-site that Jeff and I set out to become Commissioned officers. Jeff, while I was on leave, wisely accepted for both of us the invitation to apply for Commissions. But the parting from 21st Battery was a terrible wrench. We had come to love those Shankill lads and they returned our affection. I recall that on the train journey taking us from them towards another way of life, neither of us could speak until we reached

---

12 Probably confused with Tynemouth, also in NE England. Grangemouth is on the Firth of Forth. Dorman Long's steelworks were at Redcar.

2nd Lieutenant Knight

York. I think that had we spoken we would have wept. Jimmy Clyde accompanied us to the station. Our departure made it possible that our positions as sergeants could be filled by such fine men as Jimmy Robinson and Jimmy Clyde, finer blokes could not be found.

Our introduction to officer-life began in the heart of Wales, at Llandrindod Wells. The four months spent there were somewhat miserable. The regular commissioned officers made it fairly plain that they considered us completely unfit to reach their exalted status, and the regular non-commissioned officers treated us as a sort of disfranchised group that had neither the rights of the officer-class nor those of the private soldier. It was interesting to note how the English cadets, usually with less knowledge than the Irish, displayed much more confidence. This was not true of our friend 'Soapy' Hudson who, with meagre academic attainments, was sustained by a pleasant belief in his own capabilities which stood him in good stead. Jeff and I were helped through the technical and mathematical side of our training by a decent, quiet Englishman, Percy Noles, from Cheshire. He took the pair of us to his home for the weekend; I should like to meet him again. The great fear of the officer cadet was that he would be returned to unit – RTU'ed – and that he might be re-conscripted in another regiment. I remember an Ack IG threatening us with this awful fate but the indomitable Soapy Hudson explained that we had no such bothers as all Ulstermen were volunteers, and if RTU'ed would joyfully return to civvy street. How true Soapy's reading of the Army Act was, I really could not evaluate.

I think that what I felt during my time at OCTU [Officer Cadet Training Unit] was that I was not really cut out to be an officer, but, as I had got myself into this situation, I should try to make the best of it. And, in retrospect, I am very glad that I did have the opportunity to serve as a commissioned officer for a few years. That rank gave me entry to a social milieu which would have otherwise been barred to me; and mixing in that milieu gave me a confidence which I should never have in any other way obtained. All these experiences were to hurt my life, to enrich it and to lay the foundation of the great happiness and contentment which I have known in the last thirty years of my pilgrimage. They were also the basis for the supreme delight I found in French and English literature.

I cannot say that I enjoyed any part of the OCTU except perhaps the opportunity it gave me to see the lovely countryside of mid-Wales. Yet, one becomes accustomed to one's discomforts and so it was with a tinge of regret that I saw the end of training approach and that I realised that soon I should have to join a new group of people.

Jeff, Percy Moles, RIK Commissioned Officers 1941

Here I must add that fate dealt kindly with Jeff and me. At the end of the OCTU all were invited to state the location to which they would prefer to be sent; and the sensible Englishman, in nearly every case, opted for an area near his home. Not so the Irish veterans of Dunkirk. Our foolish pride prompted us to volunteer immediately for overseas service, the Far East – and in particular, Singapore! When eventually the postings were announced, the Englishmen found that indeed they had been permitted to serve near their home towns, but Second-Lieutenants Jefferson and Knight were assigned to the 60th HAA (City of London) Regt, RA, at present in Scotland, but a mobile regiment imminently poised to go abroad. But this is where Fate played its part. Lieuts Jefferson and Knight joined that regiment and began training with divisions destined for the invasion; but, that invasion, it will be recalled, was delayed and delayed and delayed, for close on three years. And the 60th regiment remained at

FROM DUNKIRK TO THE INVASION: 1940-1944

Commissioned officer with his mother on leave 1941

home. It was otherwise with our former OCTU colleagues; during those years of delay they were gradually and separately shipped to Egypt, the Desert, the Far East and Iceland, while we, the gentlemen who had volunteered for Singapore, stoutly defended Ramsgate and the Norfolk Broads. Had we gone to the East, at best, we would have been prisoners on the notorious Burma Railway. God was good to the pair of us.

We joined the 60th HAA Regt in Glasgow where it was engaged in the defence of the Pool of Gourock,[13] an anchorage for the ocean convoys. The colonel received us with anything but cordiality, wondering why his English territorial regiment had to accept two Irish officers. Still, it was a wonderful thing to be with Jeff, and though he was posted to one Battery (168) and I

---

13 60th Heavy Anti-Aircraft Regiment defended the Clyde from September 1941 to May 1942.

to another (206), we felt that we were not too far apart. In passing, I should say that the 60th at that time consisted of three batteries, 168, 169 and 206. We did not know that the 206 battery was 'attached' and came from the 58th Regt based in Greenwich. These subtle differences were lost on us.

COLLEAGUES

My introduction to 206 Battery remains fairly vivid. I arrived late at night, in the dark, at Gourock, to be greeted by a Lance Bombardier whose accent immediately intimidated me. It sounded as certainly stemming from Eton and Oxford – a change in tone from the L/Bdrs of the 8th regiment who hailed from the Shankill and Ligoniel; and I was correct in my identification, the L/Bdr in question was a son of Sir Valentine Holmes, the most eminent of the KCs practising in the English divorce courts, and had been educated at both the establishments mentioned.

Hardly had I settled in the Nissen hut when there arrived Lieut. John Newton, a man who informed me that he was the bad boy of the regiment, and that he had been transferred from one of the other batteries for constant insubordination. John brought with him a large Golden Labrador, an immense amount of expensive kit, a very superior sheepskin coat, a large supply of gin and brandy and a selection of the very best briar pipes. In these first hours in his company, he announced to me that he paid the army to keep him on and explained this statement by telling me that the amount he paid in income tax vastly exceeded his pay as a lieutenant. Why anyone could find himself in such a situation was, for me, a novel idea; at that time, as a bank-clerk, my income tax amounted to £3 per annum. Yes, John Newton and his life-style were something new to me and, looking back, something interesting and educative.

I was only a few weeks with the regiment when I was dispatched on a three week Advanced G.L. and Radar[14] course.

---

14 Gun Laying Radar was developing rapidly in the early years of WW2.

FROM DUNKIRK TO THE INVASION: 1940-1944

Now my knowledge of radio was such that I could distinguish a crystal from a valve set, and no more. After the first lecture, the course passed completely beyond my comprehension, and so, for the remaining twenty days, I sat in my place counting the minutes until I could escape from this deluge of meaningless technicalities. A man who had a fair knowledge of radio would have benefited from the course; as for me, I could only think of the criminal waste of government money which was occasioned by sending me on it. There was only one bright spot; at the end we all went to Glasgow to a restaurant called Rogano's and I was introduced to the liqueur Drambuie.

My next assignment with the 60th centred on the building and construction industry. I was called to RHQ and asked if I knew how to erect a Nissen Hut, and when I replied that once in France I had assisted in the assembling of one such edifice I was ordered to return to my battery, collect thirty men, occupy with them a site near Gourock, and from there proceed to the construction of a Nissen hut encampment to accommodate two hundred ATS at Inverkip, a small village on the Clyde. My knees nearly gave way under me as I pondered my complete ignorance of such an undertaking.

However, the army does not always act foolishly. On returning to my battery, an experienced sergeant called a parade and quickly picked out thirty men who in civil life had experience as bricklayers, joiners, plumbers and labourers, though some of the latter were a bit odd. One wee man, a Jewish tailor from Whitechapel, had never had a pick or shovel in his hand in his life; on the other side another little man was a ditcher from Buckinghamshire – he was like a mole, slowly and relentlessly he shovelled away; he could have dug a trench from one end of England to the other.

It was a pleasant period, those weeks on the Inverkip site. The mornings had the crispness of early autumn, and for me to be out in the open air in the sunshine was a delight, yet a delight always tempered by the thought "This won't last, eventually you'll have to go to face an enemy, somewhere." Gradually the camp took shape; the first hut rose complete on its foundations and I was proud as Wren must have been of St Paul's. Then one day a Brigadier (RE)[15] arrived, inspected the work and complimented us on what we had achieved. Emboldened by his words, I ventured to point out that the distance of the huts from an existing wall was two feet in error, according to the plan. To this the Brig. replied "Young man, have a bit of sense. I send out these plans and usually they don't manage to erect the buildings in the correct field." I felt better after that.

Here I should mention that as we were working from early morning to dusk, I failed to make a daily inspection of the men's billets. Then one morning, after we had been on the task for six weeks, I decided to see how they were faring. Never did I see such a shambles: beds unmade for days, empty beer bottles, blue-moulded hunks of bread and cheese, half-filled tins of stale jam and fish, cans of rancid butter; it was terrible. I should have been reduced to the ranks on the spot. Still, I did learn never to allow men to take things too easily, some check is necessary for the good of all. Yet these were as decent a crowd of lads as anyone could hope to know. They just let things slide because I was too slack.

My successor as officer I/C this encampment project was none other than that highly qualified civil engineer, Willie John Jefferson! – a solicitor in civil life, and utterly handless. I had seen nine huts erected; It was Jeff's job to bring in a water-supply from the neighbouring hills. He told me afterwards that he had enjoyed wandering those heights, but as he could not see very far, he just left the work to his able sergeant.

Eventually, the ATS camp was completed, after six months of work. Then a Queen Bee ATS arrived, took one look at the site and immediately condemned it; the girls' sleeping quarters were in too close proximity to those of the men. The huts had to be dismantled and removed to another field; but we did not have to undertake that task. The army had indeed strange ways of

---

15   Royal Engineers

FROM DUNKIRK TO THE INVASION: 1940-1944

RIK and Jack Boreham, 1980s

working, but I'll not complain, those weeks at Inverkip were a most pleasant addition to wartime experience.

It was while we were in the Gourock area that my friendship began with Jack Boreham – Jack Yelland Boreham from Esher, Surrey. He was christened Jack, and Yelland he claimed linked him to some noble family; indeed, he had the coat of arms hanging in his hallway. My attraction to Jack, and his to me, must have been of opposites. He was sophisticated, I was not; he was English; I was Irish; he was a Londoner, I was a barbarian. I think that my being Irish gave me an advantage in winning his affection; for, being Irish, it was not possible, socially, to grade me. We had no public schools in Ireland; we had no county cricket; and our accent was indefinable. So an Irishman or an Ulsterman had to be accepted just for what he was in himself. Yet beneath our differences ran a great similarity; I think we both were trying hard to be decent honest fellows despite a tendency to be rogues.

Jack, I always think of as England, their England. He had been educated at an English public school, Highgate, and was very proud of that fact. From him I learned to appreciate how important it was for a certain stratum of English society to attend such an establishment. Jack was a member of the Honourable Artillery Company, the oldest military formation in England, a member of the MCC, the Marylebone Cricket Club, and so entitled to a privileged seat at Lord's. I don't think he was a good games player but, in the best English tradition, he loved his cricket, either the local or county side holding his interest.

His work as a bank official was in keeping with this background, for he was on the staff of Messrs Coutts & Co., private bankers to the royal family. The dress of these bank officials was rather special, they all wore the long black old-fashioned frock-coat. When on rare visits to London, I would call at the Strand office to meet Jack. I was always impressed and amused by the stately appearance of the staff. Later, as I came to read Charles Lamb's description of The South Sea House I was grateful that in the 20th century I had had a glimpse, through Coutts, of what commercial life in London once had been.

To complete the picture of his conventional background, I must mention that he was a devout Anglican and for many years acted as honorary treasurer of the diocese of Guildford. In everything, he liked dignity, order, decorum and the pageantry that only England can produce.

Jack, I think, at that time, could have been classed as 'an angular character'. Few people met with his approval and therefore he had very few friends, but I learned much from being in his company. He had a sophistication and a knowledge of the world that I had not: he showed me that it was possible to be a man of the highest integrity and yet, occasionally, imbibe too much alcohol. He admitted to failings which hitherto would have damned a man of my puritanical outlook, but because they were his faults, and he was the splendid character he was, I came to see as just part of life. In short, he educated me by making me more tolerant and understanding of my fellow men and women, and of myself.

He accompanied me on my first 'adult' visit to London, and, as he had a real pride in his native city, he delighted to conduct my tour. We visited Armoury House, HQ of the HAC; Dr Johnson's Cheshire Cheese, a tavern frequented by lawyers and crime reporters; another where Jack was accustomed to have a mid-day snack. At each of these we had half a pint of ale. Now, the result of this tippling was that, as we strolled down the Strand, I suddenly felt a hot sensation on my thigh and saw smoke issuing from my greatcoat pocket – my pipe had set my coat alight. I shall never forget Jack's comment, "Paddy", he said, in a most magisterial voice, "I fear there is something of a conflagration in the immediate neighbourhood." Then too, at the lonely site of Inverkip, after the Christmas party, while inspecting the Guard, he always maintained that I ordered the rifles "To stand at ease!"

To his great disgust – that expression is not strong enough – he was heartbroken when he was informed that he was too old to accompany the 60th regiment to France and was seconded to a home defence regiment. Jack's heart was set on serving his beloved England overseas, as so many of his countrymen had done down the years. He never again wished to have anything to do with the 60th; he had tried so hard to keep fit and to be in good condition to serve abroad, and he rightly felt that he had been let down.

Jack and I kept up our friendship. During the year we phoned each other several times, especially at Christmas. He was an English gentleman, and he would consider that in so describing him, I have done him the greatest possible honour. I do so with complete sincerity. I was proud to be his friend. I owe him much; he taught me much about life.

While at Gourock, I must unknowingly have looked out at my brother Jack's convoy assembling in the pool prior to its departure for the far east.[16] We must have been within one mile of each other.

At Inverkip, in some jollification, I attempted to make a standing-jump over the back of a kitchen chair; the attempt gave me a hernia which, several months later, necessitated an operation at the hospital at the Duke of Montrose's Castle. While convalescing there, I, with several nursing sisters and other officers, had afternoon tea with the Duchess. The occasion is memorable in that the one special cake was green-moulded inside and so inedible; it became my task to fill the pockets of my jacket with this stale sweetmeat when the Duchess was not looking.

1942-44: TRAINING FOR THE INVASION

I was next sent on a regimental Officer's gas training course, in the Lake District, near Ullswater. This was a useful exercise. I could at least understand all that was being said, rather a change from my advanced radar course.

All this time there was much talk of the 60th regiment joining the invasion force. Some of the batteries went to Inveraray to train on landing-craft with the commando. I did not participate in these expeditions. However, when I returned to Scotland, after the hernia operation, the regiment was despatched in great haste to Hertford to undergo a month's infantry training. We spent Christmas 1942 in that town. I was successful as an infantry platoon commander but, on the day of the Brigadier's inspection, I utterly disgraced myself: given a platoon to command, I was ordered to take it across to a white farm house, some three-quarters of a mile distance. I was also told that there we would have lunch. My great error was to suppose that the war was suspended for the meal-break and so I led off as if we were on a normal peace-time route march.

---

16 Jack's regiment, the 8th Belfast HAA, embarked for India and Burma in Spring 1942.

FROM DUNKIRK TO THE INVASION: 1940-1944

However, we were still apparently in battle mode and were heavily engaged by the brigade staff umpires. My platoon and I were wiped out. I think we even managed the destruction of the rear van and our own guards. At the inquest in the evening, the visiting Brigadier became nearly apoplectic as he commented on my part in the general exercise. Still worse was soon to follow for, as he continued his vituperative harangue, a sergeant standing in the rear rank succeeded in accidentally firing off the rifle of his friend in the middle rank. This was too much for the Brig: he hastily jumped into his nearby Jeep and probably did not stop until he had reached the safety of the War Office. I always felt that I had been hard done by. I was sure they said that we would have lunch.

Jeff, who also took part in this infantry course, acquired a great reputation as an "aggressive, fighting Irishman" because, given any position to capture, he invariably decided to 'fix bayonets and charge'. He told me afterwards that he adopted this tactic because it eliminated the customary flanking movement which consisted usually of a run of perhaps a mile or a mile and a half.

After leaving Hertford, we were, as a mobile AA regiment, continually on the move, and frequently engaged in massive manoeuvres, in particular, Exercise Spartan. I can only give a list of the different areas in which we were stationed over the next two to three years: the Isle of Wight; Clacton-on-Sea; Ramsgate; Leicester; Cornwall to cover the departure of the American Airborne Division going to Tunisia; Bedfordshire during Exercise Spartan.[17]

I was also sent on a motor transport course at Rhyl, North Wales. This was a most worthwhile month, the weather glorious, the countryside beautiful and the training most interesting. I learned to ride a motor-bicycle and took it up and down the side of mountains, a most useful accomplishment.

I remember doing some kind of regimental training at

---

17   Exercise Spartan took place in March 1943

Ullesthorpe. There Jack Boreham strove so hard to improve his physical fitness so that he might be included in the contingent of officers to be taken overseas. Each morning he rose early to run for a couple of miles, no easy task, for he suffered from flat feet. I always accompanied him on these exercises, and, with little success, I attempted to teach him to ride a bicycle.

LONDON SOCIETY

During the years in which we waited for the invasion I travelled into nearly every part of England, most of Wales and part of Scotland. This I found fascinating and it left me with a wonderful memory of the English countryside and villages at their best and, as regards some of the cities, at their worst. I became fairly well acquainted with London's West End; I used to stay at the Overseas Club, in St James's, in the centre of the city's famous clubland. Lady Stewart of Fort Stewart Ramelton, had sponsored my membership. I'd sometimes think how strange it was that a little North of Ireland bank clerk should be frequenting, albeit only the fringe, such surroundings. I have always been pleased that my fortune led me into those paths. I would always have felt that I had been denied the acquaintance with high society had I not for a short while moved in something approaching that circle. When I did so, I learned that it had not much to offer, but my curiosity was satisfied, and feelings of envy and frustration wiped out. None of my friends seem to have been bothered with such notions.

In 'Henry IV Part II', I later came across a scene which greatly pleased me, and indeed reflects some of the innocence which still obviously affects my outlook and my memories: Act 3 Scn2.

> SHALLOW: Ha, cousin Silence, that thou hadst seen that that this knight and I have seen! Ha, Sir John, said I well?
> FALSTAFF: We have heard the chimes at midnight, Master Shallow.
> SHALLOW: That we have, that we have, that we have ...

Let the reader take note that I cast myself not as Sir John Falstaff, but as Mr Justice Shallow!

While at Clacton-on-Sea, or rather Oulton Broad site, I witnessed one night the tragic destruction of five American bombers. These planes, having dropped their loads of bombs in Germany, were accustomed to switch on their navigation lights, as a sign that they were friendly aircraft, just as they reached the English coast. On the night in question, a German fighter-plane followed them in and, as each illuminated the signal lights, shot it down. Sitting targets! The terrible situation was that we, on the ground, could see by our radar just what happened but could give the Americans no warning, nor could we even open fire against the fighter for fear of hitting the bombers. The German pilot was awarded a high class of the Iron Cross for his daring in these attacks; and I have to admit that he deserved the honour. Still, forty years later, I can recall the feeling of dismay which swept over me as I saw the flashes in the night sky and knew, that at that moment, five or six young Americans were hurtling down to their deaths.

As the invasion date drew nearer, older men such as Jack Boreham and Bruce Leslie, and Colonel Unsworth (of whom, more anon) were posted away and replaced by younger officers. Of these, two were outstanding men, Philip Foulds and Eric Christopherson, seldom seen since the war ended but whose memory lives on, most vividly. We'll come back to them later.

⚜

4 THE RETURN, 1944-45

My return to France was less dramatic than my departure from that country. My regiment, the 60th HAA (City of London) Regiment RA (TA) made up of 168, 169 and 206 batteries, landed on D Day+16 and, by that date, all danger on the beaches had ended.

The weeks before embarkation were times of intense activity and of considerable boredom. We were stationed somewhere in Bedfordshire or Buckinghamshire and occupied our days by minor exercises, physical training and 'water-proofing'. I, as the officer in charge of the troop's waggons, spent much effort in the water-proofing of motor vehicles, from gun-towing tractors to jeeps. The object of this treatment was the sealing of the internal combustion engine with plasticine and other materials in such a way that it could run for a limited period under water. The notion being that when vehicles plunged from the landing craft ramps, they would have their engines submerged for perhaps four minutes while they drove through the water to the beach. I mention all this really to record the following incident.

During this period of training, I had to waterproof a Jeep and take it for testing to a nearby encampment where there was a deep pond through which I should drive the little vehicle. Now this encampment was, at that time, occupied by the 1st battalion of the Rifle Brigade, commanded by Lt Colonel Victor Turner VC, a brother of our own Colonel. The Rifle Brigade Colonel had won his decoration in the desert in what General Horrocks later declared to be "perhaps the most brilliant feat of arms achieved by any unit of the British Army". Well, when the testing day arrived – and it was a bitterly cold one – I took the Jeep to the pond, started up the engine and drove through the pond with only the exhaust-extension and my head visible above the water. It was a very chilly business but warmth was restored to me when Colonel Turner VC, who had been watching my exploits, congratulated me with the words, "Young man, you're a hero plunging through water on such a cold day." So, at least I've been called a hero by a VC! This Colonel became the Captain of the Yeomen of the Guard[18] and officiated at the Churchill funeral in St Paul's.

As D Day approached, and of course we were ignorant of the exact date, we began to notice the front-line troops gradually moving past us on their way to the embarkation areas and ports. I recall especially noticing the men of the airborne division who had with them pieces of the lightest artillery I had ever seen. I suppose they must have been 2-pounders.

Our own time of departure drawing nearer, and all our equipment having been waterproofed, the problem arose as to how the men should be kept occupied. I gave my lads, mostly Londoners from the Greenwich Arsenal area, a talk on "Life in the Irish village of Fivemiletown" which was based on my three years stay in that important banking centre. The tale began with what I considered a brilliant opening sentence, "Fivemiletown is so-called because it is seven miles from the neighbouring villages of Clogher and Brookeborough". To still the exclamations of disbelief or protest, I added that five Irish miles were equivalent to seven English. But my worthy drivers were unconvinced and as I went on to tell them stories of the great characters of Fivemiletown, their notion that the Irish were, at least slightly, mentally abnormal was further confirmed.

Eventually, we too moved into the embarkation zone, for us, near Southampton, and no further communication was allowed with the outside world. I cannot recall anything of interest concerning that period until the actual sea crossing. We sailed

---

18 No, he was Clerk of the Cheque and Adjutant of the Guard. The Captain of the Yeomen in January 1965 was Lord Bowles.

on a merchant vessel and what lives in my memory is the picture of an endless procession of ships, moving in both directions, across the Channel; no wonder that I later appreciated the 3rd Chorus of Henry V.[19] Again, for someone of my background, it was a shattering revelation to be made aware of the tremendous material resources that were involved in this undertaking; hundreds of ships filled to over-flowing with men and equipment, and more and more to come – some organisation!

22 JUNE 1944 (D DAY + 16): LANDING IN NORMANDY

The regiment landed at the Mulberry harbour and so the vehicles landed dry-shod, and the water-proofing was not put to the test. A few wrecked assault-craft, a sunken destroyer, and the shattered beach defences stood out stark on the foreshore while a steel-network roadway stretched on the sands led us into the dunes and past the concrete gun-emplacements that the heroes of D-day had captured on landing. Near the dunes I saw my first dead Germans. They had been killed beside their machine-gun. One was a huge man, well over six feet in height; his bloated body lay by the roadside with his face half covered by the mud of a dirty gutter. Someone's son, husband, sweetheart.

Of the first days in France I have only the faintest of memories. I know we were sited somewhere near Bayeux but, as my job was at that time with the waggons, I can only remember the camouflaging of the vehicles in the hedgerows, the frightening vomiting sound of the Spandau machine guns not far off and a feeling of unreality, this feeling induced by the lack of hostile action. From some vantage point, I watched the bombing of Caen. Four hundred heavy bombers, Lancasters or Boeings, in the calm, clear light of a summer evening flew in from the north-east, unloaded their bombs in the centre of the city, and, without any apparent trouble, retired from their target having sustained no damage to themselves.

---

19 The Chorus describes the embarkation of Henry V's fleet for France.

THE RETURN, 1944-45

Shortly after this my troop was moved closer to Caen but as the city was still in enemy hands, we advanced no further than the outskirts. The waggon-lines, over which I presided, assisted by a most rubicund faced Sergeant Wyrill, lay beside a farm-cum-agricultural-implement garage. From there, at a distance of about half a mile, I saw several of our tanks engaging German flame-throwing tanks; fortunately the fight veered away from our area.

Those waggon-lines are not to be forgotten because, in a lull in our activities, we attempted to cut the farmer's wheat crop by means of a reaping machine attached to a gun-tractor; not a very successful operation and one hindered by the fact that the field was thought to have been mined. My good sergeant's name and appearance caused great amusement to the farmer's daughter. In French Sergeant Wyril sounded very much like Sergeant Virile, and he certainly had a lusty look!

Beside us, at Caen, stood a huge state prison. The walls had been breached by shell-fire and I presume the inmates had made their escape. I shall never forget wandering through that sinister building. In one cell I picked up and read a letter addressed to Convict No XXX in which his wife informed him that she could no longer wait for his release and that she had gone off with someone else; in another cell, stuck on the wall, was a cigarette-card picture of a chorus-girl, I suppose, for years, the only feminine element in the life of that prisoner. The washing facilities sent a shiver down my spine: the handbasins were arranged in a fan-like semi-circle of cubicles which could be overlooked by one warder sitting at an elevated post at the centre of the fan. That prison was a soulless place and one was glad to step out of it into the freedom of fields and sunshine.

When Caen was eventually captured, I remember making my way through the rubble of the bombed old houses, they were literally reduced to powdered dust, and entering the cathedral. The impression that remains with me is of its solidity and whiteness. William the Conqueror's tomb is in the cathedral, and I was visiting it, as a soldier, some several centuries later.

As the RAF completely dominated the sky, our role as anti-aircraft artillery was for the time being abandoned, and my troop was despatched as field-gunners to support the first airborne division which was, I thought, something of a privilege. We sited the guns just across the Orne river and canal near the [Pegasus] bridge which had been taken on D-Day by Lord Lovat's commando and beyond which the airborne troops had landed. These formations, at that time, were unable to advance and not having any heavier artillery were glad of what little help we could give them.

For the first few weeks that we occupied this site I made about my one and only wonderful contribution to the allied war effort.

While their sons were at war, Irwin's parents entertained US troops at home

Let me try to vindicate such a claim; and to do so I must explain that in my battery, it was generally held that I was a good-natured, feckless Irishman, unable or unwilling to grasp the intricacies of anti-aircraft artillery and that, in consequence, it was hazardous to entrust me with control of the guns. This was especially the belief of my troop commander, Captain Eric Kilner, a fussy little man determined to make a good show and who ate his fingernails to the quick in his efforts to achieve this aim. However, when we became field-gunners, poor Kilner was found to be entirely unable to cope, for he had no knowledge of trigonometry. The upshot was that Lieutenant RI Knight, who had managed a pass in Senior Certificate maths at Belfast Royal Academy, became the site commander at the bridge at Ranville, controlling the ranges, elevations, bearings and fuses required for the targets selected by the airborne troops ahead of us. For three glorious weeks, assisted by young Troop-Sergeant Major Williams, to whom I taught my scanty mathematical lore, I enjoyed not only the quiet satisfaction of doing well a worthwhile task but also the pleasure of seeing the wretched Kilner squirm with frustration as he watched my success in a job that was beyond his capability. I appreciate that the account I have given of this episode reveals a none too savoury side of my nature, but I hope the reader, whoever he may be, will believe me when I declare that I was goaded so to behave and so to react.

JULY-AUGUST 1944: BREAK-OUT, ROUEN. THE FRENCH

My next recollection of those times is of the break-out from the beach-head and of our exhilarating drive forward to the historic and beautiful old city of Rouen. This event occurred about ... [August 1944] and had been made possible by the crushing defeat of the German armour at Falaise by the Canadians, and by the drive, further south, of the Americans; but of these important moves we knew nothing at the time. For us all that mattered was that we were to push on with all possible speed.

The few days that followed were, for me, the most thrilling

and most satisfying of the entire war. In brilliant, sunny autumn weather we hastened on through the rich and beautiful countryside of Normandy and everywhere received the warmest of welcomes. This was especially the case when our convoy of heavy guns made its way by side-roads and small hamlets where we were, for the inhabitants, the first elements of the liberation army that they had encountered. I recall how, at the outskirts of one tiny village, I saw the curé emerge from his presbytery, take an astonished look at the road congested by our vehicles, and then, with a joyous cry on this lips, "Les Anglais, les Anglais!" he gathered the skirts of his long soutane up to his waist and fairly galloped down the intervening field to shake every hand that was within his reach. I rode a motorcycle on that part of the journey, and at nearly every cross-roads at which I stopped women and girls stuck flowers on the bike or in my uniform, I think I was even kissed! And men proffered drinks from bottles of cider or Calvados. The whole of Normandy seemed on those sunny days to be transported with delight. It was good to be alive, to see such elation and to be made to feel so good.

One evening we halted beside a prosperous farmhouse and taking the chance to air my French, I talked with the farmer and his family. They took me into the large kitchen, set me in a corner by the fire, filled me a glass of cider and then told me how, only twenty-four hours earlier a German colonel had sat in that very chair while, on the road outside, his troops plodded past, demoralised, weary and defeated, men pushing their wounded in wheelbarrows and prams. What astonished these farmers was the vast quantity of allied equipment which trundled past before their eyes: "Quels materiaux!" they would murmur, over and over again. I think they felt that such a display of wealth and strength ensured that German defeat was inevitable.

The climax of these wonderful few days came at Rouen. From the outskirts to the centre of the city, the people, lining the streets, at times in ranks of four or five, hanging out from open windows and balconies, waving the tricolours, strewing the road with flowers and endlessly cheering, welcomed us in a way I shall never forget.[20] Remember the lines from *Julius Caesar*

> Many a time and oft
> Have you climbed up to walls and battlements,
> To towers and windows, yea to chimney pots,
> Your infants in your arms, and there have sat
> The livelong day, with patient expectation
> To see great Pompey pass the streets of Rome.

Well Pompey had nothing on me!

The tremendous pleasure that I then experienced sprang, I think, from the feeling that now we had wiped out the shame of Dunkirk and that we had earned the right to some such greetings. Since 1940, we had served right through the London blitz, the attacks of the V1 and V2 rockets, the air-raids on the south and east coasts and we had played a part, albeit a small one, in the advance from the beachhead. We had, on occasion, been close enough to death. This is in no way to be considered as a claim for the appreciation properly owed to commandos, air borne forces or the infantry in general. For me there was the added satisfaction in being part of an army which helped to liberate France, a country for which I have always had a romantic or sentimental respect and affection.

The seamier side of war was also to be found in those days at Rouen. The retreating German army making the crossing of the Seine had been heavily bombed by the RAF. Thousands of corpses lay unburied on the eastern side of the city. The stench of death was heavy in the air. I did not see that terrible sight.

The speed of the advance for the time being slackened – the military historians have their different views on why or how this slowing-down could have been avoided. My section of four guns deployed at the tiny hamlet of Le Génetey, in the Forêt de

---

20 The people of Rouen in fact had mixed feelings: on 19 April 1944 the RAF bombed the city, resulting in heavy civilian casualties: 900 dead, 2000 wounded, 20,000 homeless.

Roumare,[21] some three or four miles beyond Rouen. The site, a large clearing in the forest, was a lovely spot in which to relax in those golden autumn days.

Soon after our arrival, we began to be visited by a few older persons and curious children from the village and the forest dwellings. One little brunette, aged I suppose about ten, came with the grandmother and, by her beauty, modesty and good manners, quickly won my special affection. I think her name was Paulette, and she certainly was a charmer! To her I gave my chocolate and sweet ration, and wheedled from the cooks some tins of corned meat, coffee, cocoa and tinned herrings for the old lady. They were obviously very poor and such foodstuffs were for them great delicacies. One day, Paulette made her way to my tent to tell me that her grandmother wished me to come to their home for a meal on the following evening. I accepted and arranged that they should meet me to take me to their house.

It was a tiny cottage, very sparsely furnished but scrupulously clean, with a deal table and chairs scrubbed white and a few flowers in a vase in the window. I was given the place of honour at the table with Paulette and then the old lady produced the meal, course by course. She had been the cook in some *famille noble* and the food she contrived to produce from the meagre resources was unbelievably delicious. Still, for me, the most moving moment of the occasion came when *grand'mere* announced that to celebrate the liberation and to show their appreciation of my gifts they had killed *le lapin* and we were to have it, roasted, as the centre piece of the repast. These people were poor, frugally poor as I think only the French can be, and obviously had not had such a feast for years, yet their pride and pleasure in sharing it with me was plain to be seen. Wine and coffee (from the powder I had supplied) were provided and I stayed late into the twilight with that delightfully genuine old

---

21 The Fôret de Roumare lies within a loop of the Seine immediately west of Rouen; Le Génetey is at the NW edge.

working woman and her dainty, charming grand-daughter. It was a poignantly beautiful episode.

A few days later was Sunday, and for the people of the district it was *le premier dimanche de la libération*. About ten o'clock we heard the church bells ringing, it seemed, with special fervour, calling them to Mass. Then, the service over, they came, dressed in their best clothes, the old and the young, to visit us at the guns. Some had the awkward look of simple peasants arrayed in their Sunday best; others could have been trades-people or shopkeepers; all gazed with admiration at the equipment, tried to talk to us of *les Bosches,* were delighted to smoke English cigarettes and, by the spontaneity of their manners, somehow made us feel that they were glad that we had arrived.

Yet one group aroused in me a feeling of loathing and anger. They were what I suppose one would call gentlemen farmers. Wearing well-cut jackets, silk shirts, breeches and highly polished knee-high riding boots, they exuded an air of opulent arrogance. Their carefully groomed hair, smooth well-nourished skins and cunning eyes betrayed a class to whom the war had been good. Too clever to be caught as *collaborateurs* they had lived fat on the sufferings of their countrymen. In speaking to us their main interest was centred on the question, *Les jolies poules se trovent-elles encore à Piccadilly?* These specimens of the Norman *haute bourgeoisie* for me epitomised the most unpleasant characteristics of the French people – they disgusted me! Yet, also on that gun-site at Rouen, was to be found the other France, good, noble, exquisite.

This idyllic interval – I can still smell the scent of the pine trees and see in the morning sun the dew really twinkling like diamonds in the grass – could not last. Orders came that we were to depart at first light and so as dawn broke, we were again on the road with the forces heading east. The romance of war had ended for me.

TOWARDS THE LOW COUNTRIES

After a lapse of forty years, it is difficult to recall the exact sequence of events which followed our departure from Rouen. There was a time when I might have done so but now only disjointed memories of that time remain with me.

At the start it seemed as if all units were heading for Paris, certainly every signpost and kilometre mark indicated the way to the capital. The weather remained brilliant, the roads were good and we saw no enemy except, every now and again, a batch of newly captured prisoners, one of the main sorry sights of war. In a pause on our journey, I remember turning my motorbike down a wooded lane in search of a glass of cider and fresh eggs. Coming to a cottage, I pushed open the door and entered the kitchen. It was a mean, through-other place, occupied by three of four rather slatternly women who looked guilty and frightened by my approach. I explained my errand and just then two young men, poorly dressed, slunk into the rear of the room; there was much whispering and then I heard one girl say, *Il est grade – un lieutenant!*...[22] and then I was given a glass of cider.

This brief encounter has remained with me. I have often wondered if the poor people had been collaborating with the Germans; they could well have been countryside prostitutes and now feared retribution had come upon them. Again, they may well have been just representatives of the common folk whose fate it has always been to live in an area over which rolls the flood of war and battle. If indeed they had associated with German soldiers it is not to be wondered at if they felt fear, for, at Rouen, I had seen a young woman, who had had a baby by a Boche, paraded through the streets, her head shaven as a mark of her treachery. The Resistance had a keen eye for such offenders but there were responsible French citizens who told me that many of the Resistance were new recruits to that cause, and that many such people used 'patriotism' to pay off old scores. Unsavoury acts are done in a land where normal law had broken down.

---

22   He's an officer – a lieutenant

THE RETURN, 1944-45

Paris was not to be liberated by R.I. Knight. Instead, my regiment progressed north-east towards the Channel and Belgium. An interesting occasion in this advance was a visit to one of the huge guns used by the Germans to shell Dover. This was an extraordinary installation. Each gun, one per fort, was as long as a telegraph pole and was housed in an emplacement that resembled an underground fort about quarter the size of the Belfast City Hall (a homely comparison.) The gun and control rooms were covered by a roof of sixteen feet of reinforced concrete. We were told that 200 RAF planes had bombed the forts for several days. The result of their effort was a cratered surface, at least half a mile square, which made one think of pictures of the moon's surface. The bombardment had been so intense that it had rendered the defenders punch-drunk or dazed before their surrender. Certainly, looking at that pitted ground I realised what a terrible ordeal they must have gone through. I saw there the ruins of an 88mm gun and was glad that I had never had to endure such a hammering as must have fallen to the lot of these gunners.

Not far from this area we came across one of the launching stations for the V2 rocket.[23] Tunnels, dug by forced-labour gangs, ran deep into the face of a quarry and down these tunnels ran railway lines which allowed the rocket launching apparatus to be brought to the cliff face, the rocket fired and then permitted the apparatus to withdraw into the safe depths of the earth. I should mention that the tunnels faced outward towards England. These sites were elaborate undertakings powered and lighted by electricity, with huge well-equipped workshops and each with barrack accommodation for the forced-labour gangs of workers. These rocket sites would have been a terrible danger to England for they were indeed immune from the effects of any bombing. Not far away, I saw the launching pad for a VI rocket or 'doodle-bug'. This was a very simple affair, like a turn-table

---

23 Probably the *Coupole* at Helfaut-Wizernes or the similar site at Eperlecques, both near St Omer.

for a narrow-gauge railway. It was said that as these missiles were exceedingly unreliable and given to premature explosions, the Germans forced their Russian prisoners to fire them.

SEPTEMBER 1944: BELGIUM, GHENT, BRUSSELS, ANTWERP

By the time the Belgian frontier was reached, autumn was about to begin. Our job, I think, was the protection of certain centres against air attack, but as the enemy air-force appeared to be completely depleted we had little to do. At Ghent, Harold Christopherson and I made friends with a local family who invited us to their home on several occasions; it was unkindly said of the Belgians that they loved the British soldiers and not a family but had an officer visit the home! I recall that Chris and I paid an unexpected call on these good people and found them celebrating the one-day-yearly visit of their eldest son who was in training as a Jesuit Priest, a fact of which the parents were very proud. The meal was something of a feast, but the memorable thing for me was to see the wreaths, sprays and garlands of flowers sent to the house by relatives and friends as a tribute to this young man. I found it an odd spot to be graced by the presence of a staunch Ulster Protestant!

Various duties took me to Bruges, Louvain and Namur, names that I had learned of in school history lessons. In these lands I was always conscious of the fact that I was treading in the footsteps of countless British soldiers who, down the centuries, had fought their battles over northern France and the Low Countries. And, of course, there was the Wife of Bath 'Of cloth making she hadde such an haunte/ She passed them of Ypres and of Gaunt.' A trip to Brussels was one of the highlights of those weeks. The Officers Club occupied the Hotel Foch (I think that was the name), strange surroundings for a little bank-clerk who lodged in Bell's Temperance Hotel, Fivemiletown. I have to record that the battlefield of Waterloo was inspected by the said bank-clerk. I liked Brussels; it gave me a chance to air

THE RETURN, 1944-45

my French, it was gay, and had an atmosphere which I thought must be like Paris.

Somewhere on this move northwards I investigated a huge convent that had been badly damaged by recent bombing or shellfire. As a result of my labours I liberated a good Singer sewing machine which I kindly donated to an old lady who had mended some socks for me. Nothing like being generous with other people's property. In that same convent I unearthed some rather sexy magazines; what were such items doing in such a place?

Not long after this the Canadian army, to whom we were attached, attacked Antwerp, driving the enemy to the outlying suburbs. So the situation remained for several weeks, with the result that we were able to enjoy the flesh-pots of the city centre while the suburbs remained in a state of siege. Once again, an officers' club quickly materialised in one of the best hotels, and the pretty girls (rather, the very worldly-looking women, a collection of Becky Sharps,[24] whom one might have thought the companions a few days earlier of German officers), were apparently delighted to entertain the allied liberators; but one could not help but admire their ability to turn everything to their own advantage. Antwerp was not so much to my taste as Brussels, it lacked the sparkle of the capital and for the first time I came across the Flemish/Walloon problem, a bit like our own in Northern Ireland. Antwerp in the main spoke Flemish, an unpleasant sounding language. The Flemish, who detested the French-speaking Walloons, were thought to have been more in sympathy with the Germans than with the French.

My regiment was still far from the fighting line and still there was little for us to do. I recall that I did manage to be involved in a nasty accident which occurred in the road-tunnel beneath the River Scheldt. During the occupation many Belgians had managed to hide their lorries and cars so that they would not be requisitioned by the Germans (one such hiding place I saw

---

24 A cynical and immoral character in *Vanity Fair* by Thackeray

uncovered when a farmer unearthed his motorcar from a ditch and hedge where it had been buried for four years.) When the days of liberation came these hidden vehicles were brought to light and put on the road with very little thought being given to servicing. All this I found to my cost in that tunnel, when one such lorry, finding that its brakes did not work, swung across to the wrong side and hit my Jeep head-on. I was thrown out, hit the tunnel walls and collected several large bruises. The Jeep was a write-off. Still, once again, I was most fortunate.

I must not fail to record that in the officers' club at Antwerp we enjoyed the first hot baths to come our way since landing, that is for some ten weeks. Here it was that Bobby Barham, the battery captain, a fine soldier and one whose wealth was rather beyond my range of experience, astonished me by saying that he had so greatly enjoyed his first bath, that he promptly took a second. The idea of using a bath not primarily for cleansing purposes but rather as a source of pleasure was a notion of indulgence that I had not before encountered, and I suppose it is small points like this that make up the education that came to me in my army days. At the same club, my vanity was highly flattered when a certain Captain Connelly, one of the beaux of 169 battery, condescended to approach me for the loan of (I think) 200 francs. Happily I acceded to his request, being thus persuaded that I was being accepted as a chap with some savoir faire, but I never again saw my good francs. Only later did I learn that the captain was a most proficient borrower. Again a further point of education provided by army service; as Goldsmith says 'Home-loving youths have ever homely wits'.

LATE SEPTEMBER 1944: OPERATION MARKET GARDEN, NETHERLANDS, NIJMEGEN

The next period of soldiering came with Monty's attempt to dash forward through Holland into the industrial Ruhr, an effort known as Market Garden. I must assure my reader that, at that time, I had not the faintest idea what the operation was called or what was its ultimate goal. What was very evident was the massive size of the effort. The entire British and Canadian armies appeared to be on the road and all possessed by an ardent desire to push forward with all possible speed. Hundreds of guns, gun-towing tractors, ammunition and supply lorries, heavy and light tank regiments moved relentlessly along the road, all day and all night long. Most impressive of all were the gigantic trucks of the Royal Engineers, each carrying a pontoon for bridge building, fifty or sixty feet in length; with them came 'ducks' or amphibian tanks carried on long, low conveyor trailers. The stream of traffic was kept in motion by a horde of military police who, if they considered that a vehicle was slowing the flow, ordered it from the road, or in the case of a break-down had it pushed aside by great American bulldozers. My own regiment, an insignificant part of this great procession, stretched for two miles in close convoy, giving some idea of the magnitude of the masses involved.

At some point in this forward movement, we came across the famous German fortifications known as the Siegfried Line. Now, at the beginning of the war, a popular song sung enthusiastically and tipsily by troops at NAAFI canteens and concerts contained these boastful words:

> We're going to hang out our washing on the Siegfried Line,
> If the Siegfried Line's still there!

a sentiment which sounded hollow after the debacle of Dunkirk. However, time changes all, and I well remember seeing beside the highway of our advance, a huge sign-board erected by the Canadians bearing the legend, "THIS IS THE SIEGFRIED LINE". Then, at a distance of about two hundred yards, a clothes-line stood bedecked with army shirts, socks, vests woollen and drawers woollen long, and beside it another great placard on which these words were painted, "AND THIS IS THE WASHING!" It was rather heart-warming to read the message and to remember what lay behind it.

In fields, alongside the road, tank regiments and supporting infantry awaited their orders to move; gangs of engineers and pioneers were constantly at work repairing the surface, widening corners or laying iron network tracks; indeed what stays in my memory is the picture of a massive, purposeful movement going on in dull country, beneath grey clouds, dust and mud.

It must have been about this time that it looked as if my regiment was to be halted. The reason for this was that a main bridge over, I think, the Maas river or canal, had been badly damaged by the retreating Germans and had not yet been sufficiently repaired to bear the weight of heavy equipment. The engineers had indeed spanned the river with a great pontoon bridge but they were reluctant to allow anything but the most important material to cross by this precious structure. The idea of his regiment being halted did not please Colonel Turner (whose brother had won a VC in WW1 and, as mentioned, a second had won the same decoration in the desert – we sometimes thought our CO was going for the third) – and so he sent for me! My instructions were that I should go to the pontoon-bridge commander to enquire if he would allow a HAA regiment to use his bridge. After some time I found the gentleman in question and also found that his answer was a decisive negative. This rebuff, I thought, should be grasped by me as an opportunity to show a spot of initiative and Irish dash. In consequence I consulted my map to see if I could find an alternative route. To my surprise I noted a small by-road which might allow the regiment to proceed provided that a certain small bridge was intact and capable of carrying heavy guns. My reconnaissance of that little bridge would have done credit to an Indian scout. No-one, least of all me, knew at that time where enemy pockets of resistance might still be holding out and so I proceeded with exemplary circumspection and caution alighting from my vehicle at each corner and taking a peep round it to see if the next piece of road was clear. At length, I reached the bridge and found it to be, so far as I could see, a reasonable risk. Armed with this piece of intelligence I returned at breakneck speed to the bould Colonel Turner. He seemed pleased with my efforts but, telling me to jump into his own Jeep, he said that he would himself inspect the bridge. His idea of reconnaissance was altogether different from mine; he tore along unexplored roads, whirled round corners where I always expected to be faced by a machine gun and annihilation and, after spending an unconscionable time inspecting the bridge (which I was sure was covered by sniper-fire) pronounced it sound. However, on the return journey, he called with the pontoon bridge commander, and whether he pulled his rank or met an old buddy from Woolwich, obtained permission to make the crossing. So the 60th (City of London) HAA Rgt. RA (TA) moved on. I was never on such an insecure structure as that pontoon bridge!

WINTER 1944-45: THE RHINE

Once the Dutch frontier was crossed one was aware that here was a land where the people had suffered; the fields, the houses and the people looked neglected and desolate, and while a few tattered orange flags hung from battered farm buildings, the people were in no mood to welcome any army; they had seen too much. In one town I saw a mass grave in the main car-park, still lying open. It contained fifty or sixty coffins. The story behind this spectacle was that SS troops retreating through the streets and knowing that the inhabitants were sheltering in basements and cellars, had thrown grenades through the grills allowing them to take a last revenge on these unfortunate civilians. All the dead had not yet been collected.

At a level-crossing, I saw my first booby-trap. A huge shell had been connected to the crossing gates in such a way that movement of the gate would activate the shell-bomb.

At length, my regiment took up positions around the famous Nijmegen bridge which, just a few days earlier, had been captured by the Americans and the Guards. My troop crossed to the far side and I can very well remember looking down from the Jeep and seeing how only half of the bridge roadway was, in one place, intact. The gap beyond it, with a drop of hundreds of feet to the River Naal, was spanned by a few wooden tanks [sic, probably planks]. Dutch civilians were credited with having destroyed most of the leads to the demolition charges.

It was from this location, I think, that I saw some of the airborne division – a great number of gliders and their towing plane – going to the Arnhem landing area. Little did I realise then what a terrible ordeal lay ahead for those men. My memory on this point is vague.

At this site we had two problems, trivial indeed compared with those suffered by the men of Arnhem. The guns had hardly been put into action when it appeared that something strange was happening; no rain was falling but the ground was rapidly becoming more and more sodden. Then the news came that the Germans, in their efforts to slow the advance, had opened sluice gates and were intent on flooding the area. There was nothing to be done but to withdraw.

To do so proved a most formidable task. In what seemed only a matter of minutes, the ground, a fine silt soil, turned to an ooze of sticky mud. The gun-tractors had to use their anchors, first to haul themselves to firmer ground and then from such points, trail the guns in a slithering movement across the intervening space. It took many hours to cover the distance of half a mile to the firm causeway. As officer in charge of this manoeuvre, I waded knee-deep and more, backwards and forwards through the morass and, without food and in the bitter cold of the late evening, I reached a point of exhaustion that was something new to me. As last, however, when all the equipment was safely beached on the roadway, I stumbled out of the mud. I must have looked pretty well all-in, for Bobby Barham ordered me to his Jeep and took me back to HQ where, so far as I remember, they plied me with boiling cocoa and put me to bed covered with a pile of blankets. I was done! Yet as I write these lines, I am very well aware that the soldiers of WW1 and those on the eastern front would have thought my experience as unworthy of even a mention; all honour to them.

A long and miserable winter then began. Montgomery's gamble "Operation Market Garden" had failed because the vital bridge at Arnhem had not been captured (see the fine account *A Bridge Too Far* by Cornelius Ryan) and so there was no chance of a rapid advance over the Rhine into Germany. Instead, the British army was halted south of the river and settled down to endure, as best it could, an exceedingly cold and bitter winter.

Holland in those days was a sad and dreary country. The people had been harassed by the Germans and their food ration reduced to a cruelly low level. I saw children with sores on their heads through malnutrition searching the refuse at our cookhouse bins for the chance of an edible scrap of bread or meat. We gave them what we could. The Dutch I found to be an unattractive people. Certainly in the area through which we passed they were dull, and yet so clean – even in great adversity they had a standard of cleanliness which was nearly off-putting! I used to think that they spent all their energies on keeping the inside of the house spotless and shining because outside the land swept away, dull, flat and monotonous. They are not a good-looking race; their language is harsh sounding; their girls only look graceful when they are skating on the canals. Of course, this is an unfair assessment, no country, no people look best when bitter cold and starvation is the regular order of the day. My jaundiced outlook may also have been produced by the fact that for several months I suffered from acute diarrhoea – near dysentery. This affliction defied the skills of the medical officer but he observed that once we left the vicinity of a gigantic coal dump and moved into an atmosphere free of coal dust, my troubles would end. He was proved correct.

For most of that winter, we occupied sites about one mile south of the lower Rhine. The Germans were entrenched on low hills on the far bank while our infantry were in fox-holes just half a mile ahead of us. In our dug-outs we managed to maintain small fires and to be supplied with the usual hot meals. There were no such comforts for the infantry. In the intense cold, they had to sit in those fox-holes; they dared not even smoke lest they betray their positions and bring mortar fire down on top of them; they received only one hot meal and that was when the darkness fell and allowed their cooks to move forward to them. No one like me who has served in the second or third line troops but must hold the infantry as men of a higher plane. They are the real soldiers, as Willie Jefferson used to say, 'They can have my bed any night'.

From this site our guns were used to shell the enemy across the Rhine. Each troop was allotted a number of targets and, in accordance with the prevailing theory of the time, the men had, to stimulate their interest (!), to be informed of the nature of each of them, as, for example: Target A: Crossroads: Target B: Ammo Dump: Target C: Assembly Point: Target D: Canteen: etc. It says a good deal about the British soldiers' outlook that when the order rang out from the command post, 'Ten rounds per gun; Target D. Enemy Canteen' there arose from the gun pits the cry of protest, 'Bloody shoime....bashing up Jerry's F...ing NAAFI!"

About this time, one of our officers, Captain John Newton was appointed Admiral of the Rhine Barges. At least that was the title bestowed on him by his friend, Capt Bobby Barham who declared that John had been so favoured because, in civil life, he was an underwriter at Lloyds. John, a fairly elderly subaltern, during most of his artillery career proved to be a difficult character. He was very wealthy. I remember on first meeting him he assured me that he paid the army to keep him on, a remark which he elucidated when he informed me that he paid much more in income tax than he received as an officer. (My own salary as one of the financial experts of Fivemiletown and Downpatrick was £130 per annum and I had not yet moved into the income-tax-paying bracket).[25] He always travelled with a copious supply of whisky and brandy, wore a large sheep-skin coat, and when possible was rude to anyone who crossed his path. To be fair to him, despite obvious disadvantage in years,

---

25 But see page 68

he struggled manfully to keep up with much younger men; still I fear that he was a financial and social snob who despised most of us and especially the battery commander, Major Tony Reave, a most enthusiastic young Territorial, but, in civil life, a bank clerk. It infuriated such an independent gentleman as John to have to take orders from someone younger than himself and from a man he would have treated in civil life as a menial. Not many in the battery were sorry to hear that John had been seconded to his new charge and it was not without malicious delight that we heard that, in his first trip up the Rhine, he had managed to sail his barge right through the telephone cables that connected the most advanced observation posts on one side of the river and GHQ on the other. Which reminds me that earlier in our advance through Normandy, John managed to orient his guns 90 degrees out of true line. In consequence, his first salvoes, instead of hitting the enemy, landed in the outskirts of a French village. John's comment, and it revealed much of his character, was 'All one could do was laugh or weep, and I certainly was not going to weep!' In dealing with men like Newton one was at an advantage in being Irish. Our accent defeated him as did our entire indifference to the hierarchy of English public schools and so he was unable to evaluate our social background. Still, I don't expect he gave much thought to that for he was one of the class of Englishmen who think that anyone who resides outside the Home Counties is a barbarian.

Before I leave John, I must recount one of his favourite reminiscences. During WW1 he was travelling down by train to Portsmouth with his father, a very well-to-do general practitioner. The old gentleman, just as intolerant and independent as his son, always did his best to frighten off any traveller who attempted to set foot in his first class compartment. On the occasion in question he seemed to have succeeded but, just as the train moved out of Waterloo, the guard pulled open the door and bundled in, to the irate doctor and his son, a meek-looking little man and a large suitcase. Dr Newton let the newcomer understand that he was anything but welcome and when the latter asked if he could change his clothes, Doctor Newton indicated that he could proceed to do so but such behaviour was not what he was accustomed to in a first class carriage. The little man apologised but despite the hostile atmosphere divested himself of his civilian suit and quickly donning uniform revealed himself as Admiral of the Fleet Lord Jellicoe.

John Newton holds a further corner in my memory. When travelling from Scotland to the south of England in a troop-train which lacked all toilet facilities, John decided that he urgently required to urinate, but was persuaded by the rest of us to hold on for a few moments until we reached Manchester Central where we were scheduled to stop and where, we assured him, he would find the necessary accommodation. The train however did not halt in the station but beyond and just outside it. This was too much for John. He put a foot on each seat, lowered the window and proceeded to relieve himself. Unfortunately, just at that instant, the train began to reverse and, as John was unable to halt the flow, to our great delight and to the shocked amazement of the waiting passengers, he pumped the entire length of Manchester Station's central platform.

But to return to more serious matters. Though we all believed that the war was nearing its end, that winter dragged slowly; mud, rain, snow, ice and a desolate landscape remain as dominant memories. The great German offensive in the Ardennes occurred in the month of December and repercussions of its seriousness affected troops as far north as us and certainly shook our complacency. There were stories of how the enemy, on recapturing recently liberated areas, murdered the inhabitants who had welcomed the allies.

When the German advance had been repelled, mostly by the heroic sacrifices of the Americans, especially at Bastogne, it was again possible to snatch a 48hrs leave in Brussels. My one excursion into the black market financed such a trip for me. By selling 500 cigarettes, I was able to pay my hotel bill and my café meals, certainly a bargain. Brussels at this time was a centre for such business and when the advance into Germany began that business fairly boomed. Truck-loads of stuff came daily from that country, liberated by the gallant allies. Rumour had it that a group of Canadian deserters had organised themselves into a unit, complete with CO and Adjutant, which drew pay from the army paymaster's office as well as carrying on their much more lucrative trade in the *marché noir*.

As I have already mentioned, during the winter we were occupied in shelling the enemy positions north of the lower Rhine. Our Troop Commander Philip Foulds came from Nottingham,[26] where his people ran the main music shop of that city. He was one of three brothers serving in the forces; one, an Anti-tank RA officer lost a leg in the Normandy fighting; Phil, himself, was mentioned in despatches for his excellent and courageous work as an O/P officer when we were in Holland. He was one of the finest men I met in my army days, a born leader of men: lean, active, understanding, efficient, with a sense of humour and tremendous drive. A gifted musician, he succeeded to the family business; Bruce Leslie often visited him on his forays through the English midlands.

Eric Christopherson came from Newcastle-on-Tyne; a gifted fellow, he had a first class honours degree in Maths from Durham University. He had not quite Phil's charm but he too was a splendid companion. In the section, Phil was in command; Chris looked after our gunnery problems; I acted as Waggon Line officer, and more especially, as a sort of sympathetic listener or welfare worker to the gunners. We were a good team and a happy one. After the war, Chris entered the civil service, rose to great heights, and on retirement was awarded a CBE. In those winter months, the three of us, Phil, Eric Christopherson and I combined to make a team which ran our troop both efficiently and happily; we became, I suspect, the best troop in the regiment.

Bruce Leslie joined the regiment with Phil Foulds. A much older man, he was as tough as whalebone. Early in the war, he

---

26 The text gives Derby, to which the business moved after the war.

had volunteered for the Scots Guards, but being turned down, decided to wait for his 'call-up'. Again, he was a man of great charm and moral character (all my friends were saints!). He had a marvellous capacity for drinking Scotch whisky, absorbing it without any apparent effect upon him. Bruce left the regiment with Jack Boreham; for Bruce this move was philosophically accepted. Realistically he reckoned that he had a better chance of survival on the home front, and he had a wife and bairns to support. After the war he became director of a Dundee firm selling leather belting for factories. Often he would drop in to see us in Banbridge at our successive residences, Laurencetown House, Edenderry Cottage and Rosebank.

The mention of artillery calculation drill reminds me of a brush I endured with Colonel Turner. One night when I was officer in charge of the command post, he phoned from HQ to ask me to synchronise watches. This operation ensured that all the stop watches in the regiment were at the same setting and thus an order to fire from HQ would produce salvoes that left the 24 guns at the same instant. This precaution was of the utmost importance to prevent us from firing on our own infantry if we were giving them support. I regret to say that these finer points were not known to me at the time! When the Colonel asked for my watch reading I gave a casual glance at the dial and announced the time. Then as the seconds ticked away, I realised that I had made an error of one minute. This mistake I confessed – and then the telephone nearly exploded as the Colonel indulged himself in a caustic, curt comment on the criminality of my carelessness and he very rightly humiliated me by insisting that I checked my watch with that at HQ every quarter of an hour all night long. However, I got some of my own back: when the Colonel was leaving us at the end of the war, it was decided to give him a silver cigarette case inscribed with all our signatures. I sent in my subscription, with great pleasure, but I took the opportunity to suggest that a solid silver stop-watch would make a far more appropriate gift, adding that where I came from, we had a less exacting notion of time than had the

Colonel. I was not at the presentation dinner but I learned later that the old man had been amused by my words, and what more could a jesting Irishman want?

MARCH 1945: GERMANY. ARMY OF OCCUPATION

About the month of March,[27] so far as I can remember, preparations were made on our front for Montgomery's invasion, across the Rhine, into Germany. This, though I did not know it at the time, was a titanic effort involving some thirty or forty divisions. Our contribution was to form part of the 2000-gun concentration which supported the Canadian army in its attack on the Reichwald Forest, the first ground to be cleared in the big attack. The British artillery stretched, nearly wheel to wheel, over a distance of, I suppose, several miles. From the roof of an electricity generating plant in Nijmegen, I watched that great barrage begin and continue for many hours. It was said then that this was the greatest concentration of British guns seen in the course of the entire war.

Before we left Holland, I had the pleasure of visiting my sister Bee's friend of her Switzerland days, Hanni von Zeppelin, who lived at Apeldoorn. Bee had forwarded the address and asked me to take a parcel to this young woman if ever the opportunity arose. So when, at last, the north of Holland was evacuated by the enemy, I was able to accomplish this mission. I remember so well setting out in the Jeep on a lovely sunny day and heading north across the Arnhem Bridge and then continuing down the road to Apeldoorn. The town had not suffered any serious damage and I soon found Hanni's house. I knocked at the door and was greeted by Hanni (whom, of course, I had never met) with these words: "I know who you are, you are Florence Knight's brother, you are so welcome." Inside I was introduced to Hanni's mother, a charming, regal old lady, about six foot three in height, who, sitting bolt upright in her chair, welcomed

---

27 The operation began in February 1945.

me as if I had been a prince. I recall how she told me that as a young woman she had often visited London – "delicious London, delicious Harrods" – so she expressed herself. I was able to leave them a small supply of delicacies with which the cooks had furnished me, real coffee, tinned meat and Bee's parcel. That was a most happy occasion for me. I could not rid myself of the romantic notion that I should be the representative of Liberation to these sterling people, nor cease to think of the various strands of experience that had led to this meeting of Bee's girlhood friend and of Bee's brother bearing gifts from far-off Donegal.

It cannot have been long after this that my regiment moved across the Rhine, not far from Cleves, there to begin a new way of life, that of the conquering or occupation army. A less pleasant experience.

It was a strange sensation to be, at last, among the Germans, "the people who had caused all the bother"; an over-simplification, but that's how we thought then. People avoided looking at us and, for the most part, seemed to be in a bad state both mentally and physically.

I cannot remember much about Cleves, but Osnabrück lives in my memory. The devastation caused by the 400-strong bomber raids was beyond anything I had seen or ever imagined. The main streets no longer existed but, in their place, bull-dozers had cleared tracks through the rubble, rubble which lay in mounds forty to fifty feet high. To my eyes it was as if all the buildings from Belfast's Midland Station to the City Hall had been pulverised and the debris built up on either side of a narrow road. Forlorn people climbed the piles of broken masonry searching, I suppose, for any fragments of anything that once had been their homes. Here and there, mourners had placed little bunches of flowers at places where they calculated their dead must lie. Parts of Belfast during the years 1968-81 remind me of that sight, but Osnabrück's destruction was many, many times worse.

In contrast to this depressing and horrible spectacle was the amazing beauty of towering bridges above wide valleys. We saw magnificently tended fields and forests, farm-houses that spoke of wealth and Teutonic thoroughness, and lovely little villages complete with church and spire reminiscent of tourist posters or picture postcards. I have never seen a countryside so well cared for or so pastorally beautiful.

Yet at that time any close relationship with the Germans was strictly forbidden; the policy was known as non-fraternisation and it led me into a few strange situations. The first of these occurred when the regiment took over an area from the outgoing RE unit, and I found myself in charge of the troop waggon-lines in a very splendid farm-house, the sort of establishment one associated, in England, with successful racehorse trainers. The REs had appropriated the mansion, installed themselves in all the best rooms and, following the non-fraternisation rule, banished the owner and his family to the stables in the yard. After a few days, news was brought to me that the owner, Herr XXX, craved an interview with the officer commanding – that is, with me. In consequence of this request, I held an urgent preliminary meeting with Sergeant Wyrill, and the only man in the section who knew any German, Lance Bombardier Goldstein, a Jewish tailor from London's East End. We agreed to grant the interview, and determined to conduct it in proper style.

So it was that I found myself seated at the end of a huge mahogany dining table, like a Lord of Appeal, supported on either side by my good NCOs and protected by two drivers, armed with rifles, as court ushers. At a given signal the owner, a giant of a man, and his wife were conducted in and made to stand at the far end of the great table. They then made their pleas which for my benefit L/Bombardier Goldstein translated. These were that they might be permitted to have the use of two bedrooms, and of the kitchen and that they might be assured that their property would not be destroyed.

After considerable whispered consultation, during which Sergeant Wyrill, of the choleric mien and purple complexion, scowled at the two natives as if he could scarce refrain from bayoneting them, I delivered my verdict to the effect that as non-fraternisation was army policy, they could have no access to any bedrooms or the kitchen, and that therefore they must continue to live in the stables. Regarding the third request, I told them that we had recently been informed that a brother of one of our officers had been captured by the SS and had been flogged and that as a result we were not feeling, just then, particularly sympathetic towards the Aryan race. Further, I let them know that my men, not having slept in a bed for nearly a year, would be permitted to make themselves as comfortable as possible during their stay in that house. Then, magnanimously, I assured them that I would do my best to ensure that no permanent damage was done to the fabric of the building. The couple were then given leave to retire from their own dining-room and so came to an end my brief impersonation of Montgomery, Churchill and the Lord Chief Justice. In passing, I should add that the owner expressed his distaste for the SS and, so far as I could gather, the Nazis in general, but in an attic I had already come across a Hitler Youth song-book. I suppose it must have been impossible to remain completely untouched by the heady Nazi propaganda, and equally difficult to remain unimpressed by their brilliant early successes; one can think of Irish parallels.

A few weeks later, I again found myself as a guardian of the law. This time my duties arose, paradoxically, from the necessity to protect the Germans from night attacks by the now-released slave-labourers, mostly Poles and Russians, who, we learned, had cut a few throats in revenge for past ill-treatment. Each night I set out with a patrol of about ten men to tour the district and to investigate anything we considered suspicious. One ploy, in which we took wicked pleasure, was to knock, in the early hours of the morning, at a large farm house and insist on a complete search of the building. In I would march, accompanied again by Sgt Wyrill and L/Bombardier Goldstein, and demand entrance to every room. The houses, I should add, were filled to overflowing with refugees from the bombed cities and with farmers seeking safety from the attentions of the Poles and

THE RETURN, 1944-45

Russians. It was embarrassing, and not quite cricket, to flash our torches on husbands and wives, men and women, startled from sleep, sitting up in beds, scared and usually half-naked, or to flush out wretched souls who had sought shelter in cupboards or wardrobes, yet I have to admit that there was a certain relish in inflicting just a little of the terror that the Germans had caused in the countries they had occupied. Sgt Wyrill loved it, especially, I think, the spectacle of semi-nude, fat, middle-aged women cowering in the lamp light: "B.... cows.....b.....cows" was his favourite salutation. Even then, the whole performance struck me as being a very amateur job and I often wondered if the Germans could believe that they had been defeated by such innocent, inefficient and light-hearted conquerors.

At this period, when our area had been over-run by the allies, most of the normal German public service had ceased to function. This state of affairs was sharply brought to my attention by the appearance at the gun-command post of a farm-labourer who, almost distracted, asked if we could send a doctor to his cottage where his wife seemed about to give birth to twins. Somewhat nonplussed as to how to cope with this predicament, I phoned HQ on the operational line and asked them to use their best endeavours to send us, with all speed, a medical doctor or a midwife and an ambulance. The replies were witty and mostly unrepeatable, but all suggested extreme doubt as to the existence of the farm-labourer and complete certainty as to what sort of behaviour we had been up to among the agricultural *fräuleins*. Nevertheless, the humanitarian appeal prevailed and very quickly an MO materialised from somewhere to aid the stricken lady. This little drama was enacted in a pleasant and peaceful meadow which, by all appearance, would never have had even the remotest connection with the cruelties of modern war.

Osnabrück was the limit of the 60th HAA Rgt's advance. There we remained while the victorious British, American, Russian and French armies took over what remained of the Reich. So far as I can recollect, an air of anti-climax prevailed; the war was petering out and all agreed that the sooner it was

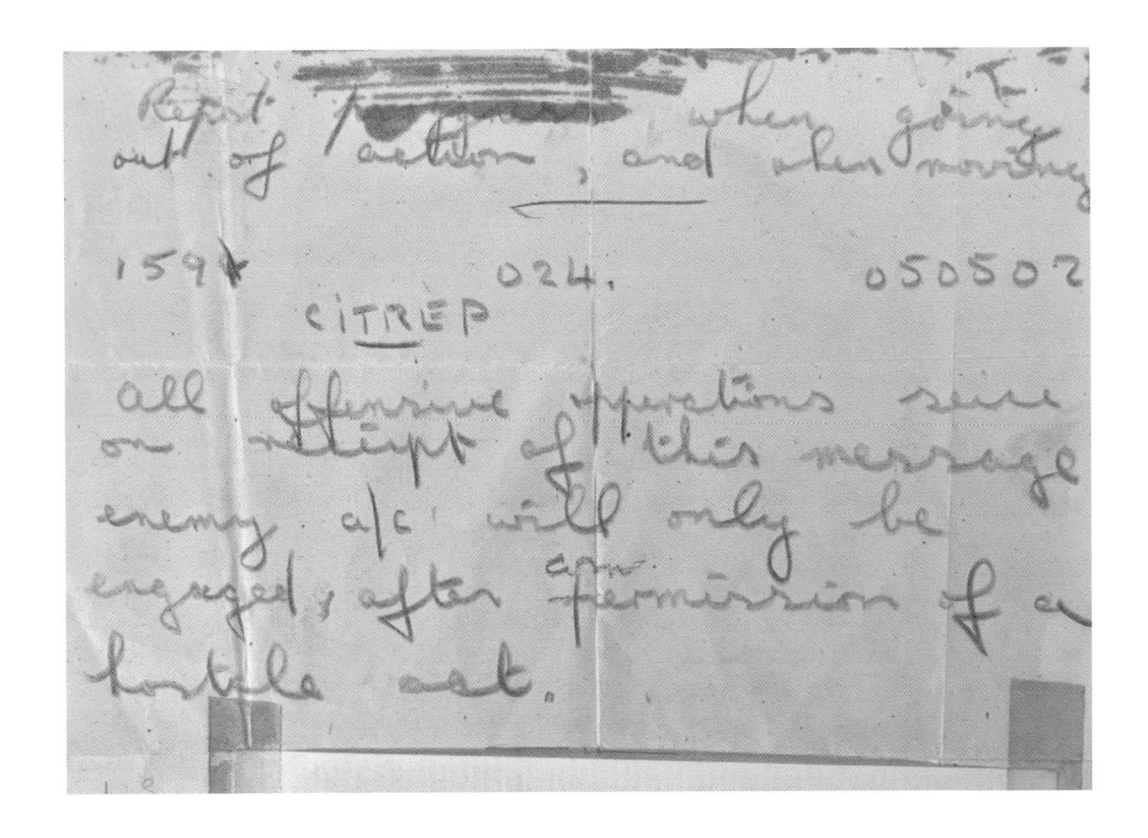

ABOVE:
Cease Fire order to E. Troop, 206 Bty 6oth (City of London)H.A.A. Rgt. (T.A.) Germany, 5th May 1945

RIGHT:
Verso of cease fire order

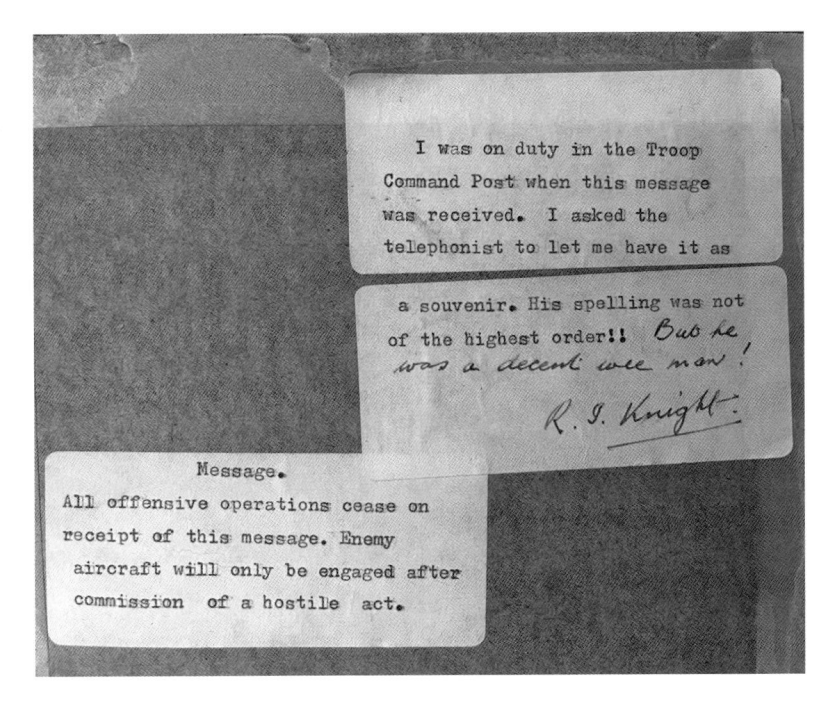

> Message.
> All offensive operations cease on receipt of this message. Enemy aircraft will only be engaged after commission of a hostile act.

> I was on duty in the Troop Command Post when this message was received. I asked the telephonist to let me have it as a souvenir. His spelling was not of the highest order!! But he was a decent wee man!
> R. I. Knight

concluded the better it would be for all, and anyway, the end was a foregone conclusion. Perhaps here I speak only from the point of someone who had seen little active fighting; men who had been in the thick of great battles may well have been filled with a feeling of elation and have really relished the days of the last great triumph. Be that as it may, my regiment was destined to take part in the last great flourish. Around 5 or 6 May 1945, orders came that, from a given hour, no enemy aircraft were to be engaged unless they committed a hostile act. This was for us the cease fire order. I managed to obtain the message signal that recorded that event for our troop, brought it home and had it framed as a historic memento. A few hours later, word came through that Monty was to receive the German surrender on 8 May at Lüneburg Heath and that he had ordered that a victory salute be fired there by the Royal Artillery. So, at very short notice, the twenty-four guns of the regiment were given the spit-and-polish treatment, rushed to the Heath and, in due course, let loose the required salvoes.

1945: AFTERMATH. NEW CHALLENGES

For me, the period after the capitulation was a time of great worry and apprehension. I had decided that I could never find happiness in my old banking job and that when I was demobilised I would resign from the service and attempt to obtain an Arts degree in the hope that such a qualification should take me into a career which would afford me greater satisfaction. The SAS have the motto "who dares wins" and while no one could be a less likely member of that splendid force, I have to say that in daring to abandon the safety of my former civilian job, and risking failure in a new venture, I won through, eventually, to an enduring happiness the like of which I had never before known. However, the months preceding the decision to embark on this adventure were, as I have already said, times of turmoil and trouble for me. My one great comfort then came to me from "The Doc" – R.L. Marshall, MA, LLD, DD, F R HistS, Professor of English and History at Magee University College, a man to whom I owe more that I can ever hope to acknowledge. I had written to ask his advice on my projected plan of leaving the bank and trying for a degree; I have his reply still. It runs on these lines: he had never been 'sicklied o'er' with the slime of common sense; each of us should endeavour to find a way of life that would bring contentment; he was quite sure that I was capable of obtaining the desired degree; and that I should be most welcome to live in his home while I made the attempt. That letter, I need hardly say, was a turning point in my career, indeed in my life. But of that I hope to tell more fully elsewhere.

To return to military matters. As the fighting had ended, a great problem arose as to how to occupy the great mass of men who, while awaiting demobilisation, still had to remain under arms. One solution was the establishment at various centres of short courses to which interested persons could apply for admission. I grasped this opportunity and soon found myself attending a series of lectures on English Literature in the University of Göttingen. In my time, I have attended Magee University College, Dublin University, the University of Göttingen, the University of Lausanne and the University of Rennes, albeit that my stay in most was brief! Still, like the Wyfe of Bathe, I can say "I have had my world as in my tyme".

Student days, as I knew them in Göttingen, were something special. We were British army officers living in vanquished territory, so we had to be treated with considerable respect. Poor students – not at all. We resided in the best hotel, were served at meal times by waiters and each morning transported to the university in a chauffeur-driven staff-car. On our arrival at street crossings, the German points policeman halted all other traffic, saluted and signalled us on our way. Returning on foot, we received the same deferential treatment; again the police stopped traffic to permit us to use the pedestrian crossings without suffering any inconvenience. It was a short-lived, wonderful, amusing, and slightly embarrassing situation in which to find oneself, or so it seemed to me. Not so, I think to several Jewish officers who attended the same university. These were Palestinian Jews, men from the kibbutzim, tough as nails. They had fought in Italy and had gained a reputation for relentless ferocity against the crack Herman Goring Division which they were accustomed to attack, at night, in silent patrols, making use only of cold steel. These men were glad to exact from the Germans every mark of respect and submission. I remember one of them telling me how he had gone into a barber's shop for a shave, and how he had enjoyed the look of terror in the man's eyes when he noticed that his client wore the Star of David badge as well as the three pips of a captain.

At Göttingen there must have been a German military hospital, for one could not help noticing the vast number of what the French so eloquently term *les mutilés*, soldiers who had lost legs or arms or both. There were so many of them that the tragedy of their affliction burnt itself into one's innermost feelings. These young man had given so much, for nothing.

Perhaps I should mention that at about this time I turned down the offer of promotion to the rank of Captain. My motives for this refusal were, as usual, mixed. First, had I accepted the new rank, I should have had to withdraw from the English Literature course at Göttingen...and my pride would not let me put myself in a position where anyone could say "He cared more for three pips than he did for a course at the university." Secondly, I did not feel that I deserved such a position; it was coming to me simply because older officers were being demobilised and not because of my own merits. The truth of the matter was that I did not feel that I was a good officer. I have never desired to control or to command; I have never felt the itch to be a leader; I have only enjoyed responsibility when it was concerned with activities in which I was sure that I would be successful, such as teaching literature, or dramatic productions. From a utilitarian viewpoint, it might be said that I was foolish not to accept this promotion; my testimonials would have mentioned the rank; but I have always been glad that I acted as I did. The wisdom of Polonius supports my stance:

A MEMOIR OF WORLD WAR II

> This above all: to thine own self be true,
> And it must follow, as the night the day,
> Thou canst not then be false to any man.

Eventually the day of my demobilisation arrived. I remember that I had to report to the RTO at Hanover, and from there begin the journey home. As the train pulled out of the station I recall looking up to the old town and particularly noting the dignity of its buildings and the beauty of its tree-lined streets. The Channel crossing, I think, was by the Ostend train-ferry.

On arrival in London, we were conducted to a large store or warehouse near Wembley, and there handed in our army kit in exchange for civilian clothing. I chose a blue suit, a soft brown hat, black shoes and a light raincoat. As I still retained my service dress uniform and greatcoat, my new outfit was placed in a cardboard box. This box became a sort of identification mark for

First reunion after war January 1946. Lindsay, Jack and Irwin with their Mother

THE RETURN, 1944-45

The Knights reunited

the recently demobbed soldier until he reached home. I travelled back to Belfast via Larne and Stranraer, first class all the way as befitted a commissioned officer. Very many years were to pass before I again enjoyed such facilities. After 78 days leave I was retired with the honorary rank of Lieutenant; the last date of service, being 23 February 1946, was recorded in the Army Gazette.

So ended my military career. I now set out to try to carve out a new and better way of life; and again, I must say that I did so with the utmost apprehension; indeed, I find it impossible to convey the feelings of anxiety and near despair that then were mine. Yet, in the end, aided by people who lived out in their lives true Christian principles, I won through to enjoy years of happiness that I never thought could ever come to me. That happiness was to begin four or five years ahead; it had to be striven for, but it came.

POSTSCRIPT, 29 JANUARY 1982

This is not a very thrilling story but it is a fairly honest one. Or so I think.

To write these pages as I have done is to give only the surface of the experiences recounted. Beneath them lay a welter of hopes, fears, frustrations, disappointments – and flashes of joy – to which only James Joyce could do justice.

⚜

EDITOR'S ACKNOWLEDGEMENTS

My cousins, Gordon and Kenneth Knight, and Janet Deehan and Mary Howie (both née Knight), for advice, memories and photographs.

The designer, Susan Waine, who as ever brings clarity and balance to a text.

Jonathan Williams, as usual, for advice.

The maps are by de Buitléir Survey and Mapping.

My wife Sue, for insisting that the Memoir should be published; and for much else.